The Thread

The Thread

Adoption Stories Knit Together by Love

Edited by K.J. Nally

ISBN: 1519113757
ISBN 13: 9781519113757

"My friends, adoption is redemption. It's costly, exhausting, expensive, and outrageous. Buying back lives costs so much. When God set out to redeem us, it killed him."
—DEREK LOUX

Dedicated to Mollie Best,
An answered prayer to the Best family

Table of Contents

God's Heart on Adoption

Father to the fatherless, defender of widows—
this is God, whose dwelling is holy.
God places the lonely in families; he sets the
prisoners free and gives them joy.
PSALM 68:5-6

~

*E*yes, big and round, stare back at you. There are so many of them; people, young and old, everywhere you look. Scanning the crowd you notice that one out of every three people has "ORPHAN" stamped on his forehead. Then you notice the faces of these orphans: desperate, alone, and without purpose. Your heart breaks for them. What they need is hope, a future, and a family!

But how... And who will claim them?

ORPHAN has at some time stamped the forehead of every person ever born on this planet. And though the opening paragraph may sound like an orphanage in a third-world country, it encompasses the world. For these orphans represent a third of our global population who have chosen a life of hopelessness, in bondage to their sin, rather than accepting Jesus' gift of salvation and being claimed 'child of God.' But for those of us who have witnessed the saving grace of Jesus Christ, we are now stamped CHOSEN, for we are no longer orphans, but sons and daughters of God the Father.

Adoption is foremost about the Gospel; lost orphans, humans adopted by God. Ephesians 1:4-8, 11 proclaims, "In love he predestined us for adoption to sonship through Jesus Christ, in accordance with his pleasure and will—to the praise of his glorious grace, which he has freely given us in the One he loves. In him we have redemption through his blood, the forgiveness of sins, in accordance with the riches of God's grace that he lavished on us. In Him we were also chosen."

God explains that with Christ we are *born not of flesh or the will of man, but born of God* (John 1:12-13). The Father loves us so much, He chose to *pay* for our adoption and then claim us as biologically His child! Even Jesus proclaimed, "I will not leave you as orphans, I will come for you" (Jn. 14:18)! My friends, the gospel is the foundation for the practice of adoption. It is the very heart of caring for the orphan!

The opening paragraph can also be read as the dire need to adopt children who—whether they are too young to know it or not—are in desperation for a stable, loving family. As Russell Moore explains in *Adopted For Life*, "The gospel of Jesus Christ means our families and churches ought to be at the forefront of the adoption of orphans close to home and around the world. And as we become more attuned to the gospel, we'll have more burden for orphans."

In the upcoming pages, you will read about burdens overcome by HOPE; stories from birth mothers who chose to sacrifice their own wants for the best of their children; couples who have given all emotionally, physically, and financially to fight for a precious child; and grown children once labeled "orphan," now a son or daughter with a hope and celebrated future.

Though each family's story differs in the road leading to adoption, every one was blessed through Bartow Family Resources located in Cartersville, GA and concludes with a similar message: Adopting a child brought them closer in their relationship with God as they experienced God's heart on adoption.

You'll also hear a couple recurring themes in Section Two, adoptive families' stories: First, no matter how we try to control our lives, God's plan is the only one that prevails! We must learn to rely on Him with every step—even when suffering and circumstances threaten to steal our joy—because He has something amazing planned if we trust and obey. As you read, the supernatural power of God is evident in every story.

And second, adoption is costly. Not meaning financially, however, it can certainly be monetarily straining. For many of these families, the adoption process was burdensome and emotional...until that glorious day when the birth certificate read Chosen with the forever parents' last name!

If you are considering adoption, don't let these difficulties intimidate you. You'll read that the trials and fears of adoption vanished at first sight of a beloved child. And, if adopting children is a reflection of the Gospel, our adoption into God's Forever Family, then we shouldn't be surprised there are challenges and battles to destroy that image. Adoption is not just adding a child to a home or fulfilling the desire deep in a mother's heart, it is a spiritual battle for an eternal soul. Through the storms, these stories showcase God's perfect provisions and extraordinary plans. Adoption can be a difficult journey, but it is an adventure like nothing you've ever experienced. Be encouraged as you read...these real life stories are God-made!

The men and women sharing their stories are all Christians striving to lead Christ-centered families. So each experienced adoption through Jesus Christ into the family of God, and the gift of legally adopting a son or daughter. The reality in both experiences of adoption is that eternal souls are at stake; lost children who need to know their Father, and desperate children who need a Christ-centered family. And in both experiences, one thing is certain: God's heart *is* adoption.

Understanding The Thread

*Tying it all Together with first hand views from
two former pregnancy center directors.*

~

*B*eing a follower of Christ breathes adventure. This adventure is bound
in obedience and at times, risk. Obediently leading a crisis pregnancy
ministry is definitely full of both adventure and risk—the greatest risk,
having your heart broken. Almost every day my heart breaks as I meet
another beautiful woman who does not see herself as valuable; she feels
purposeless. I've learned that a person's view of purpose is often tainted by
the words of man. Whatever the lies we believe, the truth for each of us is
that our value must come from the Word of God. Because the words of our
loving Creator and Father, give us confidence to correctly understand our
identity and live out our purpose.

When a woman comes in the doors of the center scared and confused, it
is holy ground for the caregiver that greets her. There is no mistake that she
walked through our doors. As we lovingly give her hope, she learns to trust the
One who created this baby… and trust Him with the future *life* of the baby.

We have heard everything from "the baby belongs to my boyfriend's
dad" to "I am married and the baby is not my husband's." The most common are "my boyfriend or husband will leave me if I carry this child" and
"I cannot possibly care for a child at this point in my life."

So, what can be done in these tough situations? In human eyes it makes
sense to "get rid of the problem." However, we view with God's eyes,

which says all life has value. So *this child* is not *the problem* and secondly, we can trust that God is always working out a marvelous plan…He sees the BIGGER picture!

At our pregnancy center, when a woman and man cannot care for the child we simply say, "Have you considered adoption for your little one?" Please hear me, adoption is *not* saying, "I do not care about this baby." Adoption says, "I care so much about this child that I am going to choose a family who will be able to provide the best life possible."

The decision to raise their child or choose a family is completely their choice; we walk beside them no matter what they decide. At Bartow Family Resources, we are not an adoption agency so we do not provide legal input, but always refer to a lawyer or an adoption agency. Our role is (and always has been) to lovingly walk beside the birth mother and adoptive family.

The thread of adoption that builds families comes from two ends, the woman carrying the child and the woman who has been praying desperately for a child!

A woman with a crisis pregnancy: "I just don't think I can go through with this pregnancy. This is a total surprise and I cannot go through another pregnancy it is just too hard! I really do not want to abort this baby, but it is really not a baby yet, right?"

A woman who desperately wants a child: "We have tried for years to have a baby. I have had two miscarriages and those were three years ago. The doctors tell us there is not any medical reason why we cannot get pregnant and have a full term pregnancy. I just do not understand why we cannot have a baby. My heart is broken."

A woman with a crisis pregnancy: "I cannot be pregnant! My boyfriend will leave me if I don't have an abortion. He will leave me! I want this baby, but I also want my boyfriend. I am so confused."

A woman who desperately wants a child: "We are so thankful for our biological child who is almost three years of age. At his birth I had to have an emergency hysterectomy. I try not to ask why because we had dreams of having at least three children. Our little boy wants a sibling. We would love to adopt a baby and we promise to love and care for him or her with all of our being."

The thread begins when two lives intersect, one who is pregnant but needs someone to care for this precious life, and one whose arms are empty waiting for a child to cherish.

I have considered every birthmother a ***hero.*** She gives nine months of her life to guarantee this little human makes it safely into the arms of a family. I have wept many tears thinking about the sacrifice these beautiful birth moms make for the good of their child. I have also wept many tears thinking about the couples rejoicing as empty arms are filled with a little bundle of joy.

When a crisis pregnancy occurs, the darkness and "what ifs" are paralyzing. Put under the light of God's truth, we can trust Him with every life and then rejoice with a new perspective. Every family that is in this book brings to light the glory of God as He unfolds His greater plan.

It has been an honor and a privilege to walk beside those that have chosen an adoption plan for their baby. It's been equally gratifying to work with the families sharing their stories in this book. We are passionate about educating our community on adoption, so there are many families who come to our center for adoption education. Then we get to see their dreams fulfilled when they begin their adventure after saying, "Okay! We want to adopt."

Thank you families, thank you adult adoptees, and most of all I thank you birth moms for sharing your amazing stories. God truly has a marvelous Big Picture!

--Cindy Smith, Director of the Relationship Center At Bartow Family Resources

There is nothing more perfect in life than knowing you are at the right place, at the right time, doing the right thing. That is a summation of my directorship of what is now Bartow Family Resources.

From the moment I witnessed the birth of my son and cut his umbilical cord (nearly 21 years ago now), my heart was stirred for adoption and I knew God was up to something very special!

As director, I had heard the heart of so many women overwhelmed with a crisis pregnancy. Their fears of facing motherhood when it seemed an impossible task—a task they were not ready to accept—was heart wrenching. My own heart broke for these women, and while they had come to the conclusion they wanted to choose life, they needed more. They needed options.

At the same time I also saw the tears and heard the prayers of other women unable to bear a child. Women who would give everything they owned to have a baby. Women asking God "Why not me?" broken and wounded beyond measure.

What started with a sweet, concerned grandmother asking me to adopt her grandson was just the beginning of referring desperate young women to women wanting a child to love as their own.

There is no way to measure the lives that have been touched and changed by the families and children involved through the adoptions completed—by the very hand of God—through this ministry. Just as there is no way of thanking the selfless birth mothers that sacrificially chose life.

God's hand has been on this Center from its inception. He has taken it from a doctor's small office to a 10,400 square foot building! He has blessed it beyond everyone's expectations and continues to work miracles daily.

I will forever be grateful for the time God used me as Director of the Center, and for the privilege of being used by Him to place much wanted babies into the arms He designed to nurture them.

If you find yourself today in the shoes of these women who were faced with an unplanned pregnancy, my prayer is that you will choose life. May you find hope and healing through these stories for what we know is a very difficult and delicate decision.

And remember this truth...God always gives His very best to those that leave the choice with Him.

--Rebecca Banks, Former Director of Bartow Family Resources

Stories from Birth Mothers

"A Birthmother puts the needs of her child above the wants of her heart"
-Skye Hardwick

Chapter 1

Christy's Story

I am glad that God worked a miracle for someone else through me.

⌐

I was seventeen and a senior in high school. Sure, I lived with my mother, but my home life was a mess. She let me do whatever I wanted. So, I came and went as I pleased. I partied; I drank, and stayed out until I was ready to come home. Many nights coming home was only long enough to get ready for school. And school was if I felt like going. Far from being an adult, yet permitted to make adult decisions.

The turning point in my life was when I discovered I was pregnant. Quickly, I sobered, as I had to figure out what to do. One thing I was certain, I was not ready or fit to be a parent. I felt lost and alone. My boyfriend at the time didn't care what I did; actually, he tried to talk me into having an abortion. But I couldn't take an innocent life. Four months went by as I thought about what I should do. During this time no one knew that I was pregnant except a few of my closest friends. As I got further along in my pregnancy, I knew soon I could no longer hide the reality of a baby growing as I began to show. I needed to talk to someone. First, I reasoned I should talk to my mother, but since we saw life so differently I knew she would not understand my hopes for this child. So, I decided the next day that I would talk to the school counselor.

Beyond nervous, I sat in front of her unable to get the words out. She kindly asked me what was on my mind. Hardly believing my ears when I finally blurted it, "I'm pregnant and I don't know what to do!" She graciously gave me her time that day. I told her about my doubts to take care of a child and that I would prefer to find someone to care of this child for me.

In my current situation, I knew providing for this child the way a parent should was impossible. And I only wanted what was best for him. Then, my counselor put herself and career on the line. She told me about a place that would help me, a crisis pregnancy center. She also told me about a family that had been waiting for years to adopt a child and if I was interested in meeting them and pursuing this avenue she would call the center and make arrangements for me to go there.

For the remainder of the day, I thought about her offer. Finally, I decided when I got home that afternoon I would tell my family I was pregnant and let them know what I was going to do. And that's what I did. My mother was distraught, but surprisingly she agreed with my decision, knowing I was doing the best thing for this child.

The next day I called the crisis center and made arrangements to meet in person. They were so warm and caring; I cannot express how wonderful and patient they were with me. The center helped me deal with my emotions and walked me through the process of how things normally worked. My fears and doubts were relieved for the first time since discovering I was pregnant.

They told me about Jennie and Eric and how long they had been waiting for the blessing of a child. Their story truly touched my heart. Arrangements were made for our families to meet. Afterwards, I couldn't have been more pleased. Jennie and Eric were everything they said they'd be and more. Throughout the remainder of my pregnancy Jennie and Eric stayed in touch. We would go out to eat or they would come to my house. They even took me to some of my doctor appointments. We quickly became amazing friends. They encouraged and challenged me in so many ways.

The pregnancy center didn't finish their job after counseling me and finding me the right adoptive parents for my baby. They counseled me throughout my entire pregnancy. Even calling just to check in on me. I knew I was not alone; they genuinely cared for *me*.

Then it happened! Delivery time. I called Jennie to let her know that my water broke and it was time to get to the hospital. What an emotional time for us all. Our hearts were filled with joy over this beautiful life. He was perfect! Yet for me, there was sadness because of the sacrifice to come. Again, I was encouraged in my grief to selflessly love my baby and choose to do what was best for him. And that's what I did.

The crisis pregnancy center along with Jennie and Eric helped me through this difficult transition. Without them I don't know what I would have done. The center not only helped me find a wonderful, loving family for my baby, but they continued to help me work through the waves of emotion that came with my decision. I wanted the best for Chandler; I wanted him to have a hope-filled life that I could not give him. How wonderful the crisis center affirmed my decision.

I'm definitely not the only woman this center has helped—this wonderful group of people have helped so many make the best choice for their child. One thing that will always remain with me from my counseling sessions was the fact that there is the same amount of people that are looking to adopt a baby as there are abortions in our world today. This is no coincidence. God has a place for every child and the Bartow Family Resources is a vessel that He uses. And I can honestly say today, I am so thankful that God worked a miracle for someone else through me.

(Thread with Chapter Three: Eric and Jennie's Story)

Chapter 2

Katy's Story

I gave him amazing parents and the best life possible.
He gave me insight and the true meaning of love.
His parents gave me peace of mind.

~

My story is long and short, all at once. It started a year ago, but yet also started six years ago. And that is where I begin.

I was young. I was a child myself when I made the decision that I wanted children. However, when I became pregnant as a teenager, I made the terrible decision to terminate the pregnancy. Scared that my life was over and that this was my only way out, I was selfish and thought only of myself in that time period. I wasn't ready for such a great responsibility, to care for a dependent human being, when in truth I couldn't even fully take care of myself. I believed in my womb was my first son. He was to be named Anthony Michael Liam. He was to be my pride and joy.

After my abortion, I carried great guilt and regret in my heart. I couldn't believe what I had done to an innocent soul. Without ever speaking to anyone about how to deal with my remorse, I suffered greatly. No one knew how it would affect me for the rest of my life. I had nightmares, and for years I saw him in the eyes of every baby boy. I began to hate myself, and grieved silently. I believed I would never have children again.

Three years later, I became pregnant again. Inside I wasn't sure how I felt, but knew I could not terminate. That would destroy everything I had worked so hard to restore. So I made the decision to keep the baby.

Years ago, I was given an old prayer box locket that I had never used. I remember putting it around my neck with a slip of paper on the inside with the words, "Lord, give me a son" written upon it. I wore it every day.

Upon the day of finding out the sex of the child growing inside my womb, I kissed the locket and begged for my son...to make up for my past mistake. But, it wasn't time, for I had a daughter.

It was my only dream to have a son. Tonka trucks in the mud and a khaki-wearing boy playing football in the front yard with friends. But I was given a princess-loving, dress-wearing little girl that I love with all my heart. For a reason, I was given what I needed, not what I wanted.

I'm not sure how I would have reacted if my daughter had turned out to be a little man. I would have tried to make up for the past, which I have now learned I cannot do. And, I'm quite certain he would have been over-protected with no room for personal growth, because I would have tried to protect him from everything humanly possible.

After the birth of my daughter, I had an IUD put in. I was unsure how mothering would affect me and didn't want to have an accidental pregnancy before I was ready.

A year later, with IUD in place, I found out I was pregnant. The situation was bad and I was terrified. With just getting the swing of how to mother a little girl single-handedly, I was unprepared for another child. My motherly instincts kicked in and I took the IUD out to protect the child growing within. I moved back home to be with my family.

In a panic, I started "Googling" ways to terminate the pregnancy at home, safe and unsafe. For a second time, I planned the only option I thought plausible in my fear.

One night while looking up these ways, my daughter cried for me from her crib. I went to her and picked her up and cried for hours while holding her and watching her sleep. I knew I couldn't do it again. I knew in that moment, I couldn't take this innocent child's life.

In those hours holding my baby girl, I knew what I would choose. I knew that there was a family that needed a child as much as I needed my daughter. I would choose adoption.

I honestly believe my one-year-old daughter made the decision for me. And it has been the greatest decision I will ever make.

My family fully supported my decision; my grandmother picked out the family that she believed deserved a child and fit my picky criteria. I tried my hardest to disassociate myself with the baby inside me. Bumps and kicks just meant I was hungry. I ignored the fact that my belly grew each and every day. I told no one of my situation, because my situation was far harder for anyone's mind to comprehend. I chose not to know the sex of the child. I opted for a C-section. I opted to have my tubes tied. And, I chose not to hold my child after *he* was born.

I will never forget the birth. I was due on November 16th, scheduled to have a C-section on November 11th. But, I had an emergency C-section on November 5th at 5:55am.

When I awoke, my grandmother was with me. The only question I asked was, "Is the baby okay?"

She replied, "He's fine. He'll be in the hospital for a few days to get circumcised."

I burst into tears proclaiming, "I had a son." She apologized profusely and left the room. She had not meant to tell me.

Later that day I met my son's parents for the first time. I had never seen a woman or man cry so beautifully. We hugged, and cried, laughed, and talked for a long time. I then realized why my grandmother had picked them, they were beautiful inside and out. I will never forget one thing she told me, "One day I woke up and felt very maternal, I knew my child was out there for me and a few days later, I got the phone call."

They have given him a wonderful life and a beautiful home. I gave him amazing parents and the best life possible. He gave me insight and the true meaning of love. His parents gave me peace of mind.

To this day, I receive letters and pictures. I cry every time I read them and see how much he is like me. I'm proud of what I have done and have no intention of hiding this from anyone anymore. His parents have blessed him and me. They do not know this, but they gave me the best present they ever could, they gave my son the middle name that will live for a lifetime in my heart, Liam. I had always wanted a son, and since the age of 12, I had wanted a son named Liam.

I do not regret my decision. I do not regret the family that is now my son's parents. I do not regret allowing two people, so in love, to be able to enjoy the ups and downs of parenthood. The only thing I regret is not holding my son the day he was born, kissing him on the forehead, and telling him that I loved him and that I was doing the best that I could for him.

(Thread with Chapter Eight: Dustin and Kori Jo's Story)

Stories from Adoptive Families

He settles the childless woman in her home
as a happy mother of children.
Praise the LORD.
PSALM 113:9

Not flesh of my flesh, Nor bone of my bone,
But still miraculously my own.
Never forget for a single minute,
You didn't grow under my heart - but in it.
—FLEUR CONKLING HEYLINGER

Chapter 3

Eric and Jennie's Story

My hopes and dreams of having a large family
were crushed and it left me devastated.
My heart desperately longed for more children. Though the pain was
unbearable at times, our hope was in the Lord and in His Word.

~

God's Word says in Psalm 23:6, "Surely goodness and unfailing love will pursue me all the days of my life." There is no way for me to share our story about the adoption of Chandler without interjecting God's Word throughout it. Just as we pursued the dream of having a family, God so lovingly pursues us. Psalm 113:9 says, "He gives the barren woman a home, so that she becomes a happy mother."

Today, I am a happy mother.

I had been told as a teenager that I might never be able to have children. By the grace of God, I have two wonderful boys, both of which are miracles conceived from Him. Hunter, our 21-year-old was born of our flesh. Chandler, our 15-year-old was born of our heart.

The "Miracle of Our Adoption" began with a prayer. We prayed and believed just as Hannah did in 1 Samuel 1:27, "I asked the Lord to give me this child, and He has given me my request." Of course it wasn't as easy as repeating this verse a few times in prayer. In fact, it was a most difficult trial for our entire family.

In August 1996, I had a complete hysterectomy. Hunter was three years old at the time. My hopes and dreams of having a large family were crushed and it left me devastated. My heart desperately longed for more children. Though the pain was unbearable at times, our hope was in the Lord and in His Word. So I clung to Psalm 37:3-5, "Trust in the Lord, take delight in the Lord and He will give you the desires of your heart. Commit everything you do to the Lord and He will help you." He was our only hope!

In January 1997, I met Becky Banks, director of what was then called the Pregnancy Crisis Center. It was a meeting orchestrated by God Himself. She genuinely cared for me and loved me through this difficult trial. My relationship with Becky was different. For some reason, she was fully convinced that our family was going to adopt a baby through the Center. For about 18 months, I waited and watched as young girls came and went through the Center. Throughout this time, we had six different adoption opportunities that for one reason or another did not work out. Ecclesiastes 3:4 expresses how we were feeling, it says there is "a time to cry and a time to laugh. A time to grieve and a time to dance."

God, what are you doing? With every opportunity to meet a girl, it was no different than thinking I could be pregnant and with every turn down, I grieved the loss. Constantly I battled the thoughts, "Why am I so discouraged and sad?" Again and again, I resolved to put my hope in God and praise Him no matter what the outcome!

In March 1998, I went to a ladies retreat with some friends. It was suppose to be a time of restoration and renewal. However, I was going away to forget about the emotional roller coaster I was on. The weekend was drawing to an end. As a fun conclusion, door prizes were about to be given away. I jokingly told the gentleman calling out the winners to draw my name because I never win anything…and I wanted a prize! The man asked me if he could pray for me about that prize. And he prayed the sweetest prayer!

When he finished, the hairs on his arms were standing straight up. He asked me how many children I had. I answered, only one. Looking me in the eyes, he said, "Ma'am, you have another one on the way. When you hold that baby in your arms and you kiss its face, you will know that is your prize, your precious gift from God."

My dear friend Donna Jones was quick to speak up and ask him *when*. His reply was soon. Genesis 21:2 became a precious verse to me, "Sarah became pregnant and gave Abraham a son. It all happened at the time God said it would." And for me…my baby was coming at the perfect time God determined.

I met Christy, a precious 17 year old who was five months pregnant in August 1998. There was an instant bond. She had layers of hurt and betrayal that were intertwined throughout her life, but at the core of it all was a heart of gold. She was far wiser than her years. Already she had planned exactly what she wanted in a family for her unborn child. Praise the Lord! We fit that description perfectly. Psalm 139:16 quickly came to life, "You saw me before I was born. Every day of my life was recorded in your book. Every moment was laid out, before a single day passed."

God had plans for this child—our child, in Christy's womb. Now, our dreams were coming true. Four months left to endure. Our focus was fixated on Psalm 112:7, "They do not fear bad news; they confidently trust in the Lord to care for them." We would wait and trust.

On December 15, 1998,
Chandler Wade Horton,
born not of our flesh
but born in our hearts,
he was longed for and wanted,
and loved from the start.
Conceived from a blessing,
sent straight from above.
Our very own son,
at last home to love.

With awe I recount that Chandler was born exactly nine months from the day that the door-prize gentleman prayed over me! We felt like Matthew 9:26 was about our miracle…"The report of this miracle swept through the entire countryside." We rejoiced, as did so many others! I pray that I will be the best mother ever to my sons and that God will be pleased with this Prize He has entrusted to us.

This is a sweet and tender part of my life, but more than the emotions it brings, it portrays an image of an all loving, compassionate, giving and faithful God. I am so grateful that He chose me for this journey. The struggle and burdens no longer matter; I would never trade my story. God is so good!

(Thread with Chapter One: Christy's Story)

Chapter 4

Scott and Cara's Story

God never left me. Sometimes, God shows His grace
through amazing and miraculous circumstances.
Sometimes He shows it through amazing people.
God chose to use both to bring me back to Him.

⁓

In 1994, I was going through the lowest time in my life. I was depressed and very angry. After seven years of marriage, I wanted to be a mother more than anything. Doctors told me there was no reason I couldn't have a child and that I just needed to be patient. My husband, Mr. Content (a.k.a. Scott), said that God would give us a child if He wanted us to have one and that life would be fine without children. Well, that reasoning only made me angrier.

Every time I saw a pregnant woman, I hurt. I became especially angry if that woman was, in my opinion, incapable of taking care of her child. As a teacher, I often witnessed children who were abused or neglected. My thoughts overwhelmed me, "How could a loving God give a baby to a fourteen year old girl or an alcoholic or drug addict!" And yet, there they were having healthy children. And there I was, childless. In my anger, I didn't feel God's presence. No matter how hard I tried, He was silent. I was devastated.

During this time, I convinced myself that God didn't love or care for me. I then turned my anger toward my family and decided that my husband, my parents, and my friends didn't care for me either. Blinded by my pain, I was ready to throw away everything and anyone meaningful.

But, God never left me. Sometimes, God shows His grace through amazing and miraculous circumstances. Sometimes He shows it through amazing people. God chose to use both to bring me back to Him. Scott was the amazing person. No matter how hard I tried to push him away, he wouldn't let me go. It seemed the more I hurt him the more he loved me.

Eventually, I agreed to go to counseling and try to save our marriage. As he came to understand my pain, Scott agreed to go with me to a fertility specialist. Now, I can see so clearly what was so invisible to me then. God was using my husband to pour out His forgiveness and grace. Just like Scott, the more I hurt God and pushed Him away, the more He loved me and the tighter He held me. God used Scott to show me the unconditional love of Christ.

During that difficult time, Scott was praying that God would show me how much I was loved. He also earnestly prayed that I would have a Christian friend who could help me through my pain. God poured out His grace again by sending me Allison and Kelly, who along with their families loved me when I was quite unlovable.

Kelly and I had a special bond because she was experiencing the same problem as me. When Kelly got pregnant and I didn't, I wanted to be happy, but I ached in self-pity. It seemed that she received God's favor and I didn't. But, she continued loving me anyway.

I've always had a personality that takes charge and fixes whatever is wrong. I was convinced that with the right doctors, the right medicine, and enough money I would have the child that I wanted so desperately. Even though my marriage was better, I was still angry with God and insisted that He answer my prayers...the way I wanted. So, I took my demands by enduring a year of surgery, several rounds of shots, and thousands of dollars for medical treatments.

In the end, I was brokenhearted. Finally, I gave up. In that moment, I gave God control of my life. I told Him to take control (as if I had any control to begin with!), even if that meant I would never have a child.

It was almost exactly a year later that Wesley was born.

I never got pregnant.

Instead, God used a sixteen-year-old girl to deliver the gift I wanted so desperately. That girl's name, ironically, was Faith. She was a young girl. Had I seen her in the grocery store two years earlier, I would have been angry that she was pregnant and I was not. Yet, when she put that baby in my arms the night he was born, I thought she was the most beautiful young lady I had ever seen. Faith and her family allowed God to use them to bless me, despite the fact that I was so undeserving. What a picture of grace.

Faith kept Wesley in her hospital room for two full days. The nurses were convinced that she would back out of the adoption. The morning came for us to bring Wesley home from the hospital, as I was headed out the door, I looked at my Bible verse calendar and found that day's verse. It was Matthew 19:26, which says, "With men this is impossible, but with God all things are possible." Faith placed Wesley forever in our arms.

Our son is such an incredible gift. And the truth is I can't imagine him coming to our family any other way. He has such a heart for God and people. His wisdom of spiritual things has always amazed me. Even when he was saved at the age of five, I could see the Holy Spirit working in his life in a way that I've never seen in another person.

I can't count how many times I've been told that Wesley is just like my husband and me. God created him to be our child. God gave him Scott's love for music and my love for photography. He looks like me. He has Scott's gentle nature. He has Faith's creativity and his biological grandfather's gift for writing. God, in his infinite love and wisdom, provided the family created for Wesley through adoption. We make no distinction between "birth" family and "adoptive" family. We are all family, knit together through God's amazing gifts and grace.

God continues to pour out His forgiving grace every day in my life. He gives me opportunities that astound me. Still, I ask God why he allows me to have such an incredible life when, such a short time ago, I wanted to throw it all away. The only explanation is grace.

Chapter 5

Doug and Christy's Story

It was an extremely hard decision for us to stop the treatments and accept the fact that God never intended for us to have biological children. So, after taking some time to relax and let the idea sink in, amazement struck! We were so excited to pursue adoption.

⁓

O ften, when we make plans, God laughs. Not because He's cruel. But rather, He knows something unimaginable is in store for us if we simply wait and trust.

All our lives my husband, Doug, and I wanted children. When we married we planned to start building our family immediately. What we didn't plan for was unexplained infertility.

Tested and treated hundreds of times…well, so it seemed! There is nothing quite like (very) early morning trips to the clinic in Atlanta on Saturdays and Sundays, *and every other day of the week* for that matter. Our life felt like a constant visit to the doctor's office.

Infertility Sucks!

Put simply, infertility sucks! It is an emotional, physical, and financial roller coaster. It's a lonely, winding, uphill road. One of the many books I read during this journey is titled *Infertility Sucks*, which included a "Top 10 List of Situations That Prove Infertility is More Annoying than Anything Else

You've Ever Experienced." For all our weariness, its humorous approach brought much needed laughter to our hearts.

My favorite on the list is #4 – *Having a Huge Fight with Your Mother-in-Law*! The book compares the two, "How they're similar: Your family's future is at stake, and possibly that of your marriage, as well. Emotions are running high and there's a lot of crying. In severe cases, screaming may also be involved. In the worst instances, everything ends in utter silence."

But it is not always the silence that is hardest. Hearing others stories about infertility and the joy of adoption or childbearing can be both uplifting…and torture. Each person's story is different, circumstances are different, treatment plans are different; no matter how similar the story, they are still different. And while we loved the encouraging stories and advice of well-meaning friends, sometimes it created more pain.

Often irritated with these comments, another quote that meant so much to me after "comforting" words were spoken: "If you, by chance, have ventured into this [book] and find yourself mortified by its contents, please bear in mind that it was not written for you. It was written for your infertile friend, daughter or sister-in-law, for whom you can never seem to find adequate or appropriate words of comfort. Next time you want to say something to her but aren't sure how or what, give her this book instead. And whatever you do, refrain from giving her your two cents at the same time. Unless you're a walking, talking fertilized egg, that's ready, willing and able to climb into her womb, affix itself there and gestate for the next nine months, she has little use for your input right now." Perhaps crass, but humorous to my frustrated, broken state of mind!

Let's just say dealing with infertility is not a day at the beach. But it was a day at the beach that kicked off our adoption journey.

Changing Directions

After almost 2 ½ years of treatments, and then being told IVF was our only hope, we decided enough was enough. Doug and I decided very early in this process that we would not pursue IVF. We decided if we reached that point, it was time to move forward with adoption. Making personal fertility plans—how far down the road of fertility treatments you and your spouse feel ethically and morally acceptable—before you're in the moment is very wise! It was time to back up and try a new path.

It was an extremely hard decision for us to stop the treatments and accept the fact that God never intended for us to have biological children. (Perhaps, this is God's plan for many who struggle with infertility…not to bear children, but to care for the orphan). So, after taking some time to relax and let the idea sink in, amazement struck! We were so excited to pursue adoption.

The Day at the Beach

When we decided to change directions, we took a spontaneous road trip to the beach. Within thirty minutes (at almost midnight!), we were on the road headed to Panama City. In less than 24 hours we sat on a pier as we watched the sunrise. That impromptu trip was complete with lounging on the beach, enjoying time in the ocean, talking (and crying a lot), laughing, and closing a chapter in our lives before hitting the road back home.

If you know Doug, it might surprise you that he came home with a tattoo of Kokopelli, the Native American fertility god, as a reminder of the journey! That trip and a chapter of our lives closed in September 2012.

After a short break we started climbing the next mountain—the one known as adoption. If you think preparing for a job interview is hard, try preparing for adoption! This mountain was so high, with so many winding roads lined with red tape and paperwork. It was a very daunting path. (But don't let that discourage you; it's so worth it!)

Our journey started by looking into foster-to-adopt, but we quickly realized that was not the right path for us. After the heartache we had already experienced, there was simply too much risk involved with this option. We felt like we were back to zero and not sure which direction to go from there. Very shortly after, a friend sent me a newspaper article about an adoption-focused event being hosted by Bartow Family Resources near where we lived in Georgia. This was a true turning point for us; we simply knew in our hearts that they would be a major part of our story.

I remember calling both my husband (he was working and not able attend the dinner) and my mom that evening and saying, our baby is going to come through this Center. Again, I imagined a much different plan than what happened; I truly felt that we would adopt from a Center client.

Despite having an adoptee in our family, this event was the first time I had been surrounded by a large group who had all been touched by adoption. It was such a blessing to connect with adoptive parents, adoptees, and adoption professionals.

At the event, God met us where we were as He taught us through their amazing resources and connected us with the precious team from the Center. Following the event, Cindy Smith shared information about adoption consultants and success stories of other families who had worked with them. Until this time, this was an option we never really understood.

While the Center wasn't our agency, we still feel our son truly came to us through them; just not on the straight road I initially imagined. After the dinner I set up an appointment to meet with Cindy for more discussion and counseling. She shared another family's story of working with Christian Adoption Consultants and encouraged us to reach out to them. Without her guidance I do not know that we would have chosen to engage a Consultant, or going with a consultant without her direction would have been much more added stress to make a selection.

Adoption Consultant and Interviews Begin

In April 2013 we signed with Christian Adoption Consultants (CAC) and began working with our consultant, Cheri. From day one, she helped guide our way every step until our final post placement visits, and she assisted us with the seemingly never ending paperwork!

For our particular adoption consultant, the first packet of paperwork Cheri gave us to complete was 94-pages! Nineteen pages of questions for each of us to answer separately, medical forms for our doctors to complete, two pages of reference questions for each of our five references to complete, and financial forms—even the dog had to have her records checked and a reference letter! You really think you know yourself and your spouse until you start having to answer all those questions! It is a surprisingly difficult task. But, we knew the reward would be so much greater than the effort so we continued climbing!

In June, we were finishing up our home study and jumped with two feet into the adoption process, known as the "preliminary interview." To apply to agencies, you must be home study approved.

So there we were, interview time! While getting our sweet dog, Maggie to the vet for her checkup required sedatives and a muzzle...I still think the most nerve-wracking part of the approval process was the actual home inspection. Anyone that knows us would agree that we have a nice home and it is maintained, so there should be no reason to be concerned about this part, or any of the home study for that matter (no fears we'd have a clean background check!).

But talk to anyone who has been through this scrutinizing, judging interview and you are likely to hear of hours of stress, frantic cleaning of every...square...inch of their house and yes, even the stereotypic, baking cookies before the social worker arrives! *Why do they never take a cookie!*

On June 20, 2013, we passed the first interview and were officially 'Home Study Approved'! During the final meeting with Cheri we got our home study finished, our family profile printed, and applications ready to go to five different agencies. It was a busy day and it was time to take the next big step in the process; we were now on the highway traveling fast towards our final destination.

After signing with CAC we attended the Adoption Discovery class offered at the Resource Center and were so blessed to meet other families
at similar points in life. The Center was our first stop after picking up our
profile books on the same day we received our home study approval. We
met with Cindy again that day and prayed over our book and journey. She
kept a copy to share if an opportunity arose, and stayed in touch as we continued our journey. Because things moved so quick for us (all because of
Cindy referring us to CAC), we did not have lots of contact between that
day and our son's birth.

As soon as we received our home study report we immediately sent
out applications to multiple adoption agencies and attorneys. Within two
weeks we were approved and were "in waiting" with the agencies.

It was time to prepare, wait, and pray. During the wait we prayed that
our profile would reach the hearts of the birth moms (and dads) who would
view it and be encouraged about adoption, whether or not they selected
us as the forever family for their baby. We were fully trusting God that He
would put our profile in the right hands!

Between July 26th and November 22, 2013 our profile was presented
to 14 birth mothers that we were aware of. On November 25, 2013 we received a call that set our world spinning! It was from Cheri, telling us that
the twelfth birth mother we submitted to had selected us to be her child's
forever family! What a Thanksgiving we celebrated with our families a few
days later, when we shared the news of *our child*!

Our son's birth parents were actually with an agency that we had not
even applied to. God was "laughing" at our plans! This agency worked
with our consultants for referrals, and Cheri received his case. Despite
not being a 100% match to our criteria, she passed the case along for us
to consider. After much prayer and consulting with doctors, we decided to
present our profile to the birth parents.

As nerve racking as the home study process was, preparing for the first
conversation with the amazing couple that had chosen us was unbelievable.
We researched questions to ask and tips for handling the call and of course

had instructions from our consultant and the agency representing the birth family. When it was time for the call, we had two laptops, two note pads, and three phones ready with lists of questions and were prepared to take notes. Over zealous? Maybe, but we were prepared! To relieve the pressure the *Jeopardy* theme song played in the background as we waited impatiently for the call.

All of the worry and nerves were for naught—as soon as they answered the phone it was as if we had known this couple for years. It was a supernatural conversation that became the foundation of our current relationship.

The Birth Story

Our soon to be son was due in January, so we knew we had very limited time to prepare, however we were still leery of getting excited too soon. While we wanted to rush out immediately and decorate the nursery, we held off on making any major arrangements. Slowly we began clearing out and preparing the room that would be his nursery. We shopped for a crib, other furniture, and essentials.

Guess we should have moved a little faster, because the crib was still sitting in the back of our truck and the paint wet on the walls when our son decided to make an early arrival! We knew he was coming a few weeks before his due date…but not this soon! We were just beginning the arrangements to meet the birth parents and reserve temporary housing where we would stay for the delivery through the ICPC (inter-state adoption) process.

As we were finishing the nursery and making final preparations to depart for our expected time away from home, we received a call from our birth parents saying labor had started and they were headed to the hospital! That really sped up our packing process! In less than an hour we had the car loaded and were on the road, hoping to arrive before the baby.

Unfortunately, it was not meant to be. Thomas arrived just over two hours after we received that first call. We were literally speeding down the highway when our phone pinged with a text message revealing the first photos of our precious son!

He was just over six hours old when he was placed in our arms. That was December 12th, just 18 short days after we were officially matched, and about six months from submitting our agency applications.

In April 2014 we were blessed to finalize the adoption of our sweet angel in the presence of his grandparents and great-grandmother. For the first time in many years, Mother's Day was a day of joy! I celebrated my first Mother's Day as a mommy to a wonderful, happy, energetic little boy. And Thomas has kept us on our toes every day since that miraculous day!

We remain thankful every day that we discovered Bartow Family Resources, and everyone associated with the organization. And that God had a different, amazing plan for us. Our thread started with the Center, connected us to CAC, then to the agency, and finally to our son.

After the first of the year in 2014, the Resource Center began hosting monthly *Taco Tuesday's* for adoptive and foster moms. As a brand new adoptive mom this was amazing for me to connect with others who had gone before me.

Then, when Thomas was a few months old we went back to an Adoption Discovery class hosted by the Center. This time we were the speakers encouraging others! We shared our story from an adoptive parent prospective. Now with God's vantage point, I can truly say something unimaginable was in store for us!

God's smallest new star

Chapter Six

John and Becky's Story

*When you have your best-laid plans, expect God to get in
the middle and mess them all up for good. That's what
He does. Once He's turned everything upside down,
it turns out better than you could ever imagine!*

~

O ur story does not begin like everyone else's, you see we were not looking to adopt. Our job raising our three girls was about finished, and
the plan was for me to start traveling with my husband on some of his
international jobs. But that wasn't Gods plan.

As a little girl I was always intrigued with the stories of a baby being
left on the doorstep. Somewhere in the back of my mind, I felt like I would
be one of the *lucky ones* that this might actually happen to. But, life went on,
with no special delivery on my doorstep. I got married, we had our three
girls, and life got too busy to think about fairy tales any longer.

In 1975, I married the man I had prayed for when I was sixteen. I didn't
enjoy dating. Dating a guy and breaking up a few weeks later when I realized he wasn't right for me, sounded pointless and wearisome. So, at sixteen I began praying for the man God had for me, and graciously, it wasn't
long after that God brought John into my life.

Two years into marriage we had the little girl I always dreamed of. We
called her Sunshine. She was bright-eyed, cheery and always smiling. Our
plan was to start trying again when she was three, so we took the necessary
precautions needed to implement our plan. Again, God's plan was different.

When she was only ten months old I knew something wasn't "right," so I went to the doctor. He was convinced I was pregnant again, but I assured him it was impossible due to the little device he had implanted only a few months earlier. He was right; I was wrong! Just seven months later we were blessed with not one but TWO baby girls. They came early because the doctor didn't know there were two and thought I was overdue because of the measurements, and induced my labor. They were in NICU for a month. We named them Brandy and Candy. God had doubly blessed us! Our girls were two months early and only 4 pounds each, but they were perfect gifts from God!

Candy had some complications and we were told she probably wouldn't live. If she did, she would have serious problems for the rest of her life. A few days after delivery, she dropped from 4 pounds down to 3 pounds. She couldn't eat and needed surgery. For the first time in my life, I felt out of control. *I* could not cause her to live; *I* could not cause her to be normal.

How would she respond to her identical twin sister being normal when she was not? How would Brandy feel her whole life if her twin did not survive? (I knew the answer because my twin did not, and I did not want that for her.)

For the first time in my life I truly humbled myself, crying out to God to save my baby's life. I tried making all kinds of deals with God, but ultimately I knew that God was no 'deal maker.' Finally, I surrendered. It was all I had left to do after crying every tear my body could muster up.

I knelt before Candy isolated in NICU. Wires and tubes in every direction, machines constantly (and annoyingly) beeping, sick babies all around; and with a heavy heaving heart, I gave her to God. I promised Him that even if He chose to take her home, I would still raise the other two girls to adore Him.

That was my moment. That was my Isaac on the mountaintop experience. In that moment, I knew exactly how Abraham felt surrendering for sacrifice his beloved son. His son that meant more to him than life. I too loved this tiny baby girl more than life itself, but I knew her future was out of my hands. I had to put her back in the hands of the Father and be submissive to His will—whatever that would be. That moment is still the hardest thing I have ever had to do.

In just a few short weeks, God began working on Candy in miraculous ways. At six months she was completely healed. Something her doctors had assured us could never and would never happen. She began to develop normally right alongside of her twin, and was soon walking at 10 months. She laughed and played like every other child. I knew God had chosen to let us keep this beautiful, happy baby girl.

All three girls grew in love and stature. They loved Jesus, church, and everyone they met. They were everything I could ever want and more. Brandy and Candy were also very funny and kept us laughing every step of the way.

Throughout the years, all three prayed for a baby brother. Their father and I guaranteed them of the impossible, but still they prayed. They prayed and prayed, never relenting.

The girls grew into beautiful young women. When they went to high school I took a job as the Director of the Women's Resource Center in our town. It had previously been the Pregnancy Care Center, but had all but died.

The children's director at church was doing pregnancy tests in the church bathroom and ministering the best she could. That *was* the Center. No building, no volunteers, just "Peggy" doing tests.

God had bigger plans for Cartersville and the Center. The church asked me to direct it. They gave us a small house the church had previously used for Sunday school classes. I commissioned local services to donate carpet, paint, countertops and other items, and we turned it into a presentable ministry. Local physicians donated tests, several sweet ladies volunteered and we were in business!

As we ministered to young girls who found themselves with unwanted pregnancies, I began to question what we should do after the baby's birth. We educated the girls that this baby was in fact a living human being created by God. With this newfound information most chose to abandon the idea of abortion. But what about the ones that chose to carry to term, but could not raise their baby?

At the same time, I was confronted with many dear friends in my life that wanted a baby desperately but could not have one. Agencies were outlandishly expensive and there were so many wonderful couples that wanted a baby but could not afford the fees. The answer was clear. Mind you, we were *not* an adoption agency, nor did we pretend to be. We simply referred the girls to needy, vetted couples. It was *always* the girl's choice, whether to keep the baby, go through an agency or meet with couples in the community who were praying for a baby.

Leading up to and even after taking the job as director, I was bombarded with signs of foster care. It seemed everywhere I went I was faced with a foster care sign. They had been placed by the Division of Family and Children Services (DFCS) in various places within the community, and contained information about becoming a foster parent. I prayed often about this and felt the timing just wasn't right. After all, I had the three girls I was raising (mostly alone since John traveled so much), I was the director of a growing ministry that was time consuming, and I was very active in my church. I taught eschatology classes and classes on spiritual warfare. I taught Sunday school and was on the Women's Ministry Team. How could I fit in another child? I just couldn't fit it into *my* plan.

One afternoon I received a call from a friend I had served with from a previous church. They were an older couple and I knew they were raising their granddaughter who was my girls' age. She asked if she could take me to breakfast the following morning, she had something she wanted to discuss with me. Of course I was happy to meet with her.

The next morning we met over coffee and breakfast and she explained why she was raising her granddaughter. She explained that their daughter, Sarah, had gone off to college years earlier and discovered cocaine. Although she came from a great home and was raised in church, she got in the wrong crowd and never found her way out.

With just three hours short of having her degree in psychology, she left school and never went back. She soon became pregnant with Ashley.

She tried to care for her but the drugs interfered. Her parents stepped in and took charge of her daughter at the age of four. Several years later she became pregnant again. Same song. Her cousin had lost their only child in a car accident, so they adopted her second little girl.

Now their daughter was pregnant again. She was seven months along, and was incarcerated. She was caught with someone who had drugs in the car. Sarah had a long rap sheet, so she was drug tested along with the driver when they were arrested. She was also given a pregnancy test.

The judge ordered it because he knew personally knew her and had lost a niece to cocaine. He did not want to take any chances of this baby being subjected to drugs in utero. She did not know she was pregnant, the test came back positive. (She later confessed to me had she known she would have aborted.) The judge ordered her to serve the entire pregnancy in jail so she could not get to any drugs. God has always had His hand on this special young man.

So here we sat, over coffee, and Lee was asking if I would consider keeping this baby for five years. Sarah was also wanted in a nearby county for similar charges, so it would be about five years total that she would be incarcerated.

Naturally, I needed to pray about this and discuss it with my family. The girls were ecstatic and my husband was totally excited as well. So after feeling peace during time alone with the Lord, I told God "so this is why all those posters were in my face?" And I chuckled as I called Lee to tell her "yes"!

I went to jail to meet Sarah. Things went well and I began to get excited over having a new little bundle of joy in our home. We were required to take special classes and would be made the baby's legal guardians until further notice from the courts.

It was customary for me to go through labor and delivery with girls from the Center, so when the time came for Sarah to deliver, I coached her through delivery. I cut the umbilical cord and was the first to hold this beautiful perfect baby boy. I was instantly in love. He was adorable.

Sarah however was released to go home, so she went to her parents' house, with the baby. I went to visit the next day and she told me she had named the baby Matthew Corban. Matthew was "a gift *from* God" and Corban is "a gift *to* God." She found it in the Bible.

Sarah "mothered" Matthew for a few weeks, but soon became restless. She brought him to me on several occasions explaining she had a doctor's appointment, but then did not return for several weeks at a time. DFCS soon got wind of it and Matthew was put in our custody while she was to complete an 18-month parenting program. Sarah failed to show for random drug tests and was sent to boot camp. (The other county never came after her, so she was released after Matthew's delivery).

While in boot camp, the DFCS lawyer informed us that she would be ending Sarah's parental rights to the child. Either we could adopt him or he would be placed in Foster Care.

I could not fathom the latter, so we chose to make him our son. We met with Sarah and she signed the adoption paperwork. In our state the birth mother has ten days to change her mind, and on day ten she did just that. However, after meeting with the DFCS lawyer, Sarah understood she was losing her rights either way. If she allowed us to adopt Matthew, she would at least know where he was. She conceded.

On September 5, 1995, we officially welcomed Matthew Corban into the Banks Family. Matthew has loved baseball from day one. He even received the MVP award his senior year of high school. Today he is enjoying being a junior at Lee University and is a wonderful, handsome young man. We are so very proud. God has truly blessed us. All because three little girls prayed for a baby brother...and knew their God was bigger than any impossible circumstance.

Remember, when you have your best-laid plans, expect God to get in the middle and mess them all up for good. That's what He does. Once He's turned everything upside down, it turns out better than you could ever imagine! Thank you GOD!

(Thread with Chapter Fourteen: Matthew's Story)

Chapter 7

Rick and Carey's Story

Do something great God…and just let us be a part of it!

~

*A*s a newlywed couple, we assumed that life would be like a storybook: a beautiful wedding, cozy house, pets and kids, and a life of bliss. So when we found out we were pregnant, the joy and anticipation of our first child (and the first grandchild) consumed us for months. Shopping and assembling baby furniture, doctor's visits, showers, receiving many crocheted blankets…everything was progressing just as you would expect. In a matter of days we would be welcoming our daughter! We could never imagine how the next few days would change our lives.

Just two days from our first daughter's expected due date, on July 29, 2004, we arrived at the doctor's office for our last checkup. During that routine visit, the doctor sent Carey to the hospital for some additional testing. We assumed this was normal. But, little did we know that in the final days of this pregnancy something had gone terribly wrong.

Sitting in the hospital, we listened to doctors saying things like: "I am sorry, but there is no heartbeat" and "there is nothing we can do for the baby, she is gone, now we need to take care of Carey." WHAT? What just happened! What does a full-term, stillbirth even mean?

Over the course of the next two days Carey was induced and worked through labor and delivery. We held our stillborn daughter for a few brief minutes before saying 'goodbye.' The doctors had no explanation for what had happened and an autopsy revealed no cause of death—family and friends were shocked. We were devastated, our hopes and dreams were crushed.

We had a baby room ready at home, a bunch of diapers, and tons of little dresses. And now two days later we are signing paperwork to have our daughter buried. The numbness that set in was overwhelmingly painful. Could God really let this happen? *Why God? Why us?*

We had experienced so much over those nine months, and we're now walking out of the hospital empty-handed. As we drove home we kept looking back at the empty car seat. Arriving home, we opened the front door, cried, and then made the painful walk back to her room. It was silent. And it was so hard.

We had all sorts of books telling us what to expect when you are expecting, but there were no books to tell us what to do now. Do you close the door and hope the pain goes away? Or do you open the door and pray for healing?

We opened the door. It may sound like we were spiritually strong, but in those moments we were broken, angry, and our faith was rocked to the core.

The next few years were filled with doctors' appointments: there was an early miscarriage, more meetings with specialists, then multiple IUI fertility treatments, and even a few months of acupuncture. In every case doctors told us "you are in good health, this should work!" And then, with each subsequent meeting the same message, "we are sorry…don't give up." We tried to put on a strong front that we were okay, but we were exhausted and felt like we had done all we could.

Then, sitting in a church revival in the fall of 2007, we listened to a message about Abraham's faith and obedience to God. Abraham loved his son Isaac so deeply. He didn't understand why God was asking him to sacrifice his promised son. We sat there imagining how broken Abraham's heart must have been as he walked up that mountain. And then the preacher's words broke our own hearts: to truly have faith in the Lord is to "lay your Isaac down at the altar and trust the Lord."

Sometimes the things you love the most you have to hand back to God, and you must trust His plan even when it doesn't make *any* sense. *Okay*

God, you have our attention, having a child is our "Isaac." We are laying it at the alter—what do You want us to do now? God's response was clear, and just two words, "Trust Me."

Over the next few months, God placed numerous adoption stories in front of us. We met people who had adopted, were adopted, whose spouse was adopted, or who were planning to adopt. Looking back it was comical, as we found ourselves still saying, "Come on God—we are trusting you, please tell us what you want our next steps to be!"

When Singer-Songwriter, Steven Curtis Chapman's adopted daughter was tragically killed in an accident, the news article laid on our coffee table for weeks as we continued to pray, "We are still waiting Lord...what are we supposed to do?"

One Sunday morning a pastor shared his testimony, which included his own story of being adopted. He shared that when he finally met his birth-mother, he didn't ask why or harbor resentment. Instead he told her "thank you for loving me enough to place me in a loving Christian home." On the way home from church that day, I turned toward my wife at a stoplight and said, "I think God may be telling us to adopt." She cried. And then said, "I have prayed for months that your heart would also be open to adoption."

Okay God, we got the message. If this is our path, we will walk it. But we were scared and had no idea where to begin. We had many questions. The director of Bartow County Resources invited us to join a class taught at the center called, Adoption Discovery.

In eight weeks we learned about domestic and international adoptions, the financial options with adoption, and the legal process. We met another couple. We shared experiences and fears. We created a profile...and waited. Within just a few weeks we thought we might have made a connection that would open a door to adopt. We quickly found ourselves in an emotional rollercoaster that ultimately led to a closed door. Hurt and disappointed, we couldn't help but think, "Here we go again."

At some point our prayers changed. Rather than constantly asking God why this was happening, or continuing to tell God what we needed, our prayer simply became, "Do something *great* God…and just let us be a part of it."

Soon after, we were called with the news that a birthmother selected our profile. We didn't talk to her…we didn't meet. The truth is we expected another let down. The Center's director reminded us, "she has chosen life…and chosen you. It will be okay." There were months of waiting, and months of silence. Convinced this too would fail, we started planning a "get-out-of-town" vacation. That's when we got the call…a little before 2am on March 7, 2009. "Wake up! Are you ready? The birthmother is in labor, you need to get to the hospital."

Shock. We just lay in bed for a few minutes. But in the quiet, things started to make sense. We thought we were unprepared, but the door to the baby room we opened five years earlier was still open. That room was still set up for the daughter we planned to bring home from the hospital five years ago.

At 5:15 am we stood outside the labor and delivery room wondering what to say to the birthmother on the other side of the door. At that moment we felt really small. We walked into the delivery room, and for the first time we laid eyes on the birthmother. She looked at us, smiled, and said, "thank you, you are a blessing—here is *your* daughter." We were speechless.

All of our fears were gone. The fear we had about bonding—gone in 0.3 seconds. We held her, fed her, and took pictures with the birthmother. Then we called our parents! Not wanting to get their hopes up if the adoption fell through, we never told them about this coming baby. The phone rang. "Please come to the hospital to meet your granddaughter!" WOW!

That evening we all spent time together with the birthmother and family members taking pictures, and learning more about their family and all the events leading up to that day. We learned about her decision and commitment to choose life, and the fact that she had never waivered in her choice for us to be the parents of this little girl. Those are cherished moments.

Over the next few weeks, we worked with the NICU nurses and doctors, talked with hospital social workers, talked with an attorney, tried to figure out how insurance for all this would work, and signed all kinds of paperwork. We learned about adoption benefits offered by employers, and learned about details of family law. The day finally came when our daughter was released from the hospital and we could take her *home*.

Four months later we stood in front of a judge and celebrated together as the adoption was finalized. Carey and I talk openly about adoption with our daughter. We love sharing our story to encourage others.

As we look back we can see how this is so much bigger than just our family. When we reflect back on God's perfect timing, from the time our hearts were opened to pursuing adoption to the time we walked into the hospital to receive our gift, it was right at nine months!

There are so many lessons we learned: We learned that God desires to reveal Himself to us, even using hard situations, all He asks is for us to trust Him. We learned that every adoption story is special and different. We learned through our own trial to be sensitive to others that don't have children, because they may be aching with that same burden. We learned that the fears we had about bonding and finances, God was already in control of the details (i.e. Cara was perfectly created for our family, even sharing characteristics of us both, and an employer benefit paid for the entire adoption). And most importantly, we learned to rely on God's Word as He directed us step by step on this adventure.

Five years earlier, God took Lauren Elizabeth before her first breath. We experienced nine months of pregnancy, a delivery, and were left with empty arms.

Five years later, we held Cara Faith for the first time just three hours after her birth. We rejoiced in her life, gave her the first feeding, and fell in love with this bundle in our arms. God heard our plea for a child. Yes, there was a gap—1682 long days—but you can trust that God will not leave lose ends untied. He will complete His work for His glory and our best. God is Great!

Chapter 8

Dustin and Kori Jo's Story

Adoption is not just adding a sweet child to our home,
but fighting a spiritual battle for the LIFE of an eternal soul!

~

The Lord reminded us: *God's timing is always perfect; it is without delay!* Still the tears of desiring to be parents and being lost in the confusion of *why not us, Lord?*, came often. However, in our faithlessness, our Good and Loving God is always faithful. He reminded us that He has blessed us in so, so many ways and cares deeply for our hurts. He is going to allow us to be parents, in His perfect timing, without delay.

After three years of marriage, my husband, Dustin, and I decided to go off all forms of contraception. Having personal convictions about using a birth control pill, we decided while driving to visit family in Pigeon Forge that I would toss my remaining pills in the trash. It would be God's timing to expand our family. We surrendered and waited excitedly for God to bless us with a baby.

One year and three months passed—still no baby. Thoughts of infertility started rising. My gynecologist suggested tests and possible fertility medication; but we were only 26, we weren't opposed to medication, but I wasn't ready to go down that road. We prayed for God's blessing of a child. During that time an emotional game of tug-of-war pulled to overthrow my contentment. Many friends announced the news of their pregnancies. With excitement I congratulated them, but once in the solitude of my home, wept softly from the fears and broken-ness lodged in my own heart.

Winter had settled in and we celebrated our fourth anniversary. Our hearts were content waiting on the Lord; still emotions teetered to steal our peace. For the last couple of weeks I was feeling strange, I was moody and there was a dull ache on my left side. I called my doctor fearing I had an ovarian cyst. They told me if the pain wasn't severe that I didn't need to come in immediately, but to take a pregnancy test in a few days.

Days passed, and soon I discovered I was pregnant. We were going to have a baby! And I believed this baby growing in my womb was a boy. Even as a little girl, I always dreamed of having a son first. Since he was so small we nicknamed him, Lil' Bean.

Nine weeks went by and I was feeling so good. We joked that maybe there wasn't a baby in my "belly" because I didn't feel pregnant. Sure, I was tired and ate everything in sight, but I felt great. And never before did I feel so beautiful. Perhaps for some women motherhood just happens, for others there may not be a desire to have children, but for me…*I was created to be a mommy.*

Excitedly, we arrived at the doctor…it would be Lil' Bean's First Picture. As we sat in the room waiting for the doctor, we gave each other a high five and then pumped the air three times toward Heaven, giving God three high fives because this was His perfect work, not ours. We had determined from the first day God blessed us with our baby to have "open hands." This was God's little one, entrusted to us to raise. The doctor came in and talked for a while about what to expect and hospital protocol—then it was time for "Baby's First Picture."

Silence. *This isn't what an ultrasound was supposed to look like*, I thought. Where was my baby? The picture was white with only a small black circle. No heart beat. The doctor didn't need to say anything, we knew. And our hearts broke. We lost our first child on February 25, 2011.

On Sunday, October 2, 2011 it would have been our baby's due date. When we lost our baby, we cried to the point of exhaustion. It was so sweet falling in love with our first child. It gave us a small glimpse of how God loves us and how His heart must break when people die without knowing their Father; miscarried for eternity.

Months turned to years still without the longing fulfilled of holding a son or daughter in our arms, but God continued to whisper hope to our exhausted hearts, "Come to me, you who are weary and burdened, and I will give you rest."

In the days mourning the loss of our first baby, I felt the Lord speak to me. This time He quietly told me we would have a baby in 2014. Whoa! I definitely tucked that one in my heart. First, because every month I prayed we were pregnant; secondly, because why would that year be anything of significance; and finally, it just sounded strange! I know Acts 17:26-27, that says: "From one man [God] made all the nations, that they should inhabit the whole earth; and he marked out their appointed times in history and the boundaries of their lands. God did this so that they would seek him and perhaps reach out for him and find him, though he is not far from any one of us."

I knew God had the exact times for when we were to be parents, because those children were to be in this world at their perfect, God-ordained time. However, hearing a specific year seemed too mysterious. Months went by and I was still not pregnant. March 2014 went by, which I knew to be the last month I could get pregnant to have a child born in 2014. So, I figured I heard wrong.

One night, Dustin came home from his seminary class later than normal. We often had moments of sharing our longing for a child, crying in each other's arms. The night before had been one of those nights. When he got home I was already reading in bed. He came by the bedside carrying a Wal-Mart bag. Giving him a strange look, he pulled out a set of newborn onesies. His eyes filled with tears and he said, "Choose one to put by our bedside. Every time we see it, let it be a reminder that God has called us to be parents and one day he will bless us with a child to love." We again cried in each other's arms. Many of our friends and family knew how much we desired to be parents, but none could understand the depth of pain in those long moments of striving to trust our Faithful Father.

Even while we dated, Dustin and I have always talked about adoption as being part of our family plan. We believe adoption shows the beautiful picture of our Father's love for us—adopted sons and daughters. As many couples, we just figured we'd have a couple biologically, adopt a couple... and who knows have a couple more! With medical tests showing nothing physically wrong with either one of us and eight years of marriage, 12 years being together as best friends, we had an incredible foundation for raising children. Perhaps God wanted us first to adopt little ones that need a mommy and daddy? So, we focused our parenting dreams on adopting.

Dustin's family lives in Cartersville, and his cousin, Paula Best encouraged us to meet with Cindy Smith who is the Relationship Coordinator for Bartow Family Resources to talk about adoption. Our talk was exciting and encouraging. After meeting Cindy over a warm country dessert at Cracker Barrel in November of 2013, we got busy working on our home study. It was completed in March 2014. We waited.

Late spring 2014, the Lord stirred my heart to believe our baby was on-the-way. I made a visit to a woman in our church who recently lost her baby at birth. She asked if we knew anyone that needed a lot of breast milk! Yes, we did...Us! Then other amazing women began donating milk in anticipation of our baby's arrival (about 8-months worth!). Soon after receiving milk, God began whispering to my heart that we were having a *boy*. I remember sheepishly telling the ladies in our Bible study that I thought we were having a baby boy.

About a month later, God gave me the name "Jaden" in the middle of a sleepless night. In the morning, I told Dustin; he loved it! In Hebrew, "Jaden" means, *God has heard*! Just a few weeks after that on July 18th, we received a call from Cindy. We were chosen to be the parents of a little boy to be born in November. I could barely talk on the phone I was crying so hard. I remember Cindy telling me, "I'll call back tonight when Dustin's home!" Probably because she couldn't talk to me through my blubbering! When I hung up, I fell to my knees in thankful sobbing! I was a *mommy*!

This blew us away. Our longing to love a child was coming true! Realizing that Jaden's birth mother had to conceive him late February, just about the time I was thinking God couldn't possibly gift us our child in 2014.

Early in the adoption process, the Lord told me to trust Him, rest in Him, to bring our baby boy home. God's words were true. From the very day we received the call, God settled our hearts to decorate the nursery in a nautical theme. Ships, lighthouses, and the ocean. I just thought it was cute and calming, but God knew that this would be a difficult journey, one with stormy days rocked by our circumstances.

Again we would need a constant reminder of His words. Without ever knowing we were having a boy or that the nursery was themed nautical, a friend felt God tell her to buy me a sailboat bib for our baby. She said she couldn't leave the store (she tried twice) because God kept telling her to buy it for me. The day I learned about her feeling God tell her to get the bib, was the day we thought the adoption would fall through. A simple bib reminded me of God's promise...to trust Him to bring Jaden safely home.

The following Sunday, our church family prayed over Dustin and I, Jaden, the birth parents, and the fears with our adoption. A friend from church went home and asked the Lord how she could encourage us. God said to paint.

The next week she came with a painting. She explained that she didn't know why God told her to paint this scene, but she felt she must be obedient. She had no idea of our nursery theme or the words the Lord had already spoken to me. When I looked at the painting, I gasped and then cried in sheer amazement at the Lord's love for me, His child.

The Lord told her to paint a picture of a stormy nautical scene. Through the fog and haze the houses and people on the shore can barely be made out, even so the lighthouse keeps shinning as a beacon of hope to guide those lost at sea. The Lord gave her this vision to encourage us to pray in faith and "believe that God has already answered." Through our confusion of those circumstances making the adoption all but impossible, God encouraged us not to lose hope, but trust His guidance, "our Lighthouse." God is working in our lives, our baby's life, his birth parents' lives, and countless others…even with the fog of uncertainty, He will not only bring our baby home, but allow us to impact many other.

In August I quit my job to finish writing my first book and most definitely, to prepare for Jaden's arrival! Jaden's due date was November 16th, but his birth mom, Katy, was scheduled for a November 11th C-section. I thought this date was exciting because for years every time the clock read 11:11, I would make a wish God would bless me with a child! Since we lived almost eight hours away, we planned to leave two days before to have plenty of stress-free travel time and get all needed supplies at the store after arriving. Well, again God's timing is often not ours…but perfect! On Wednesday, November 5, 2014 at 5:55 am (his Nana's birthday…much better than my clock superstition) the most beautiful, perfect baby boy was born to us.

At 6:20 am, as Dustin and I were sitting quietly in our bed having a Bible Study, my phone rang. That is when I realized I missed an earlier call…it was Cindy! Every time her name popped up on the screen anxiety filled my heart! There were some difficulties over the last five months and I knew she was meeting with Katy in the next few days to make sure everything was ready. All I could think was…*Why was she calling!*

Timidly I answered, and in the sweetest, calmest voice she said, "Hey Kori Jo, you may want to get on the road because your baby was just born." AH! My baby, my son! You have never witnessed a scene as what took place in our room over the next thirty minutes. Crying and giggling we threw what we needed in bags, took turns getting ready as we packed the car, and hit the road by 7 am! Not sure how, but we arrived at the hospital in a little over six hours!

Walking into the hospital was the most surreal experience of our lives. But laying eyes on our son was a moment only God could create. I wept in awe; Dustin starred in shock. He was perfect. So amazing, we called him our angel baby. Jaden is our immeasurable gift and chosen son. He is the calmest, most beautiful, and sweetest child ever!

Jaden's biological grandmother spent some time with us in our hospital room the day he was born. She held him in her arms and then looked at

Dustin and me. I will never forget her words. "Well, he really doesn't look like either birth parent. He looks exactly how God created him to look. God created him just for you." Katy knew we agreed to give Jaden the middle name, Liam, to honor her greatest dream of having a baby boy with that name. Though we were planning a different middle name, we quickly agreed to Liam because it means "Mighty Warrior." We joke that our son's full name is, "*God has heard* and brought us a *mighty warrior* for His Kingdom!" Katy had decided not to meet us, but changed her mind the day after delivering him.

In the most emotional, epic moment we entered her hospital room. She was so young, so small. In that moment, my heart overflowed with love for this girl. We cried in each other's arms. She then told us, "I'm not sure why this all happened, but God chose me to have your baby. I will always love Jaden, but I know he is with his parents." It's funny how true those statements are. No one ever asks us if Jaden is adopted, though we love sharing his story. He looks so much like his daddy, has his mommy's brown eyes, and an outgoing, silly personality of both; he fits our whole family as he *was* created for it! I've told so many people, I feel as though I've birthed him. Perhaps that's in part because he's been a labor of love for years. And he is 'biologically' ours…a baby boy created in the womb for our family.

Our birth mother is our hero. She has loved Jaden in the best possible way, by giving him the best life possible. She chose life and was determined for our adoption to go through, even with difficult legal circumstances concerning the biological father. Adoption has been no less emotional than miscarriage and unexplained infertility! A great lesson we learned through this process was that adoption is not just adding a sweet child to our home, but fighting a spiritual battle for the life of an eternal soul!

And it was a spiritual battle…not only for Jaden's life but our trust in the Lord. At times legal issues overwhelmed us, as we pleaded with God to finalize Jaden's adoption! As our adoption took a little over a year to finalize, the Lord reminded us that just as it takes months and years for some of his children to "finalize" their adoption into his family, Jaden's adoption finalizing was no less miraculous, no matter how long it took!

And with this understanding, I stopped asking God, "why." *Why* it took so long to get pregnant, *why* we miscarried our first child, *why* there were so many legal fears during the first year of Jaden's adoption, *why* the biological father disappeared before signing consent, *why* it took so long to finalize his adoption, and even as Katy asked, *why* she even got pregnant!

Instead, I stood amazed at God's sovereignty. Yes, a perfect and beautiful child was born to fulfill the desires of a couple desperately wanting children. But, it wasn't just about his adoption, as incredible as it is. It was about the "bigger picture"...the one only God can see.

Because of the circumstances of our adoption God used us, used our "Mighty Warrior", to share the Gospel with Jaden's biological parents and countless others. In God's perfect sovereignty, He showed us His concern not only about people being adopted for *life*, but for *eternal life*. He made a way for our family to be knit together with perfect strangers, so that through Jaden's adoption, they could hear about being adopted into the family of God! That blew us away—and filled our hearts with joy at God's marvelous love for all His children.

Today we want to shout that our God is faithful. And as Paul said in scripture, "I have faith in God that it will happen as he told me." Now a year old, it's still hard to believe our CHOSEN son is really here! Jaden is a community baby—prayers and prayers from hundreds of friends and family eager for his arrival (and the adoption finalization). A friend wrote a letter to Jaden at his birth. She said, "Never before have I seen any baby so wanted, so prayed for, so loved. You are surely blessed."

We've learned even though Jaden is in our arms, there will always be fears and anxieties over Jaden's life, that come with the title "mommy" and "daddy." Just as we did with his adoption, we must trust the Lord, because He loves us and desires our best for His Glory!

We pray for God to bless us in the future with more children—brothers and sisters for Jaden. Now after watching in awe how God perfectly placed Jaden in our family, our prayers are filled with anticipation for *who* these children will be...for God's greater plan! And we'll trust Him for each whirlwind of adventure!

Nothing has changed since that first night I held Jaden close to my heart. Tears still come almost every day, the response of complete fulfillment. Because of the Lord's perfect work, we can now rest. For our Longing Fulfilled is here!

(Thread with Chapter Two: Katy's Story)

Chapter 9

Scott and Amy's Story

*Saying that God's plan is perfect doesn't mean His plan
is easy. Or comfortable. God's plan, when fulfilled in
the lives of willing hearts, is all about HIM.*

～

In August of 1997, our lives lay before us like a blank canvas. Scott had just proposed after we'd spent the summer apart serving as summer missionaries. There was so much hope and anticipation for what God would do with our lives. We spent the following four months planning and preparing for a Christmas wedding, but also planning and preparing for a marriage—a life together. We spent hours in premarital counseling discussing every aspect of married life, from finances to the size family we might like to have. Even then, adoption was in our minds. We might like to have two or three of "our own" and then adopt, we thought. That seemed like a wonderful thing to do—a great plan.

If only we'd known what God had in store.

The first five years of marriage went exactly according to plan. We finished college while Scott worked as a youth minister and I taught preschool. Promptly after my graduation, we left the comfy nest (a home and job in my hometown) and embarked on a great adventure. We moved across the country and served as missionaries in Cheyenne, Wyoming for two years.

It was the best thing we could have done for our marriage. We learned to rely on each other and became each other's best friend. Our mission assignment ended in August of 2001, and we moved to Cartersville, Georgia where Scott had landed a job teaching high school history and I would teach elementary school. We bought our first home and settled into a wonderful community only an hour's drive from family!

Soon after moving to Georgia, we decided to try to get pregnant, and by New Year's we were expecting our first baby. The pregnancy was picture-perfect, and the following August I gave birth to our beautiful baby girl, Rylee Grace, just a few months short of our fifth anniversary... right on schedule!

Rylee was a near perfect child—sweet, obedient, loving! We thought we had this parenting thing down! We dreamed of having several more just like her! When Rylee turned two we began trying for a second child.

This is where the story started to veer off the path we had mapped out for ourselves. Months came and went, and there was still no second child. At first, the waiting was a minor disappointment, but as the months continued to pass by, frustration turned to heartbreak. Eighteen months into what seemed like an endless cycle of hopefulness followed by disappointment, we began to wonder if maybe we should consider adoption *now*.

We certainly weren't letting go of our dream of having more biological children, but maybe God wanted to change up the order we had laid out early in our marriage.

Having no idea how to even get started, we began researching agencies. I called the agency used by one of the few families I knew who had adopted. We set up a meeting, but to my complete amazement, I discovered I was pregnant just days before that meeting. I cancelled with the agency, and marveled at God's incredible timing!

Three months later, at my second doctor's visit, I received the heart-wrenching news that our baby's heart had stopped beating. I was devastated. That day my outlook changed. I finally admitted that I could not control the events of my life or the way our family would grow. Over the months that followed, Scott and I took a step back and started really seeking God. I surrendered the plans I had made for my family.

This "surrendering" of my plans and the waiting that followed were exactly where God wanted me so that I would be ready when He said,

"Move." I learned so much during that difficult time. My life is really not about me or my agenda or my plan. My life is about loving and honoring God. It's about obeying God because of my love for Him. It's about pointing others to Him through my words and actions. I needed to come to the end of myself to really understand that.

Six months after my miscarriage, God began to gently lead us toward adoption again. Through His perfect timing and guidance, we met the adoption consultants who helped facilitate the adoption of our son. He was born only a few weeks after we began the process!

Our son's adoption was a domestic infant adoption. It is also considered "open" because we have maintained contact with his birth parents through pictures, letters, and emails. We were able to meet his birth parents the night before he was born, and we will always cherish that opportunity to connect with them.

The relationship we have with our son's birth mother, in particular, has been very meaningful for me. As an adoptive mom, sometimes there is a tendency to feel defensive about my position as this child's mother. Opening myself to her heart for this child and her grief in letting him go has changed me. My son has already asked if I'm his "real mom" (a question adoptive parents both expect and dread). My answer to him was that he has a birth mom and a mom. And we are both *real*.

Scott and I don't share our son's ethnicity, so hearing his birth parents' thoughts on raising a child of mixed race was invaluable to both of us. It would make things easier to just say race doesn't matter, but that isn't really true. If race doesn't matter, it's only because we have never faced discrimination because of the color of our skin. We want to equip our son to the best of our ability to love who he is—made in the image of God, but also to be prepared to handle issues of racial discrimination.

Open adoption sounds scary to many adoptive parents. Circumstances in each adoption are different, and the level of on-going communication with birth families will vary. But we are thankful to have maintained openness for our son's sake. God brought them into our lives and He brought us into their lives *for our son*. We were the answer to each other's prayers. I want to honor God through that relationship. And when our son is older, if he desires a relationship with his birth family, I don't want him to have to choose "them or us." I want him to know that he can have both.

God graciously answered our prayer for a second child through adoption. But until this point, I pursued adoption for *me*. I wanted a baby. God used the adoption of our son to open my eyes to His heart for the fatherless. In the two years following Jackson's adoption, two of Scott's brothers adopted children through the foster care system. I saw the great need for adoptive families and once again, God began to guide us toward HIS path toward our next child.

Having two nieces and a nephew who had been in the state foster care system, we decided to take the necessary classes to foster/adopt. We went through weeks of training and paperwork to complete a home study. Our hearts were open to the child God would bring into our family. While we were waiting for the process to be complete, I also spoke with my friend Cindy, who works at Bartow Family Resources and helps connect birth mothers with private adoptions. I gave her a profile book with pictures of our family and a letter to a birth mother—not really expecting anything to come of it. I only gave the profile book to one person, fully believing that our next adoption would come through foster care.

After several months, just before we were approved to begin fostering, I got an unexpected call from that friend. To my shock and amazement, she told me that a local birth mother, whose baby boy was due in just over a month, had seen our profile and chosen us to parent her baby! I was... well, let's say "cautiously optimistic." Scott and I joyfully agreed to move forward, but also agreed not to tell anyone just in case it fell through (as if dealing with that heartbreak without the support of friends and family would have made it easier).

We knew it was getting "real" when I got a phone call at work from the hospital asking for our insurance information and wanting to know if we wanted our son circumcised after the birth! That's the day I decided to let my boss know I "might" need some time off very soon!

Just over a month after we received the phone call about this baby, we got the call that he was on his way. It was a Wednesday night, and I finally got the courage to tell one friend at church about the possibility of this adoption. She was holding her newborn daughter, and I told her I might be about to have a new baby…later that night!

We excitedly arrived at the hospital the next morning to meet our precious son. Originally, his birth mom had requested to keep the adoption closed. This meant we would not meet each other or exchange any information. Having an open adoption with our first son, this was a foreign idea, but I wanted to respect the wishes of this person who was giving us the most incredible gift in the entire world.

When we arrived at the hospital, we learned that our son's birth mom had changed her mind and decided to meet us. I was glad, but nervous at the same time. What do you say to someone who means so much to you, but whom you've never met? When I walked into her room, my fears were gone. We embraced each other and cried together in what will always be one of the most sacred moments of my life. For the second time, God was blessing me through the sacrificial love of another. Her decision to choose life for her child meant the fulfillment of a dream and the answer to years of prayer.

Within a year after our third child's birth, I knew God had someone else for our family. I always thought I would have four children. When we experienced infertility, I wondered how on earth that would ever be possible. With each adoption, I felt there was no way we'd have the resources or emotional strength to go through it again, but each time God planned for our family to grow, He made a way. And He let me know. I keep a prayer journal, and I can go back now and find several times over the last nine years when I wrote that I felt "expectant." I just had a feeling that God was stirring something in me, and planning something big.

This time, I really had no clear direction. Our hearts were extremely burdened for orphans, but that was about all I had to go on. One day, I watched a television show called "An Adoption Story" about a family who adopted several children from an orphanage in Guatemala. I was intrigued by the story, so after the show I called the agency the family used, which happens to be in Georgia. The lady on the phone told me the Guatemala program was closed, but after questioning me about our family, suggested that I speak with their China coordinator because the China program might be a good fit for us. I thought this was God's way of closing the door on my idea, but decided to call for some information about China anyway. I relayed all the information to Scott and we agreed to pray.

We prayed for God's direction for over a year. At a women's retreat one weekend, I knelt on a huge floor map of the world. I put my hands on China and prayed fervently for God to give us a desire for the child He had for us, and to lead us to China if that's where he or she was. In early June of 2011, we agreed that God was drawing us to China and began the process of an international adoption, and fifteen months later, we finally met our fourth child—a two year old little girl from Jiangxi, China.

One thing that we feel is evident through our adoption journey is that God's plan is perfect. That sounds so cliché, and is much easier to say three years removed from the emotional roller coaster of infertility and adoption. It didn't feel perfect during those many months of negative pregnancy tests. It certainly did not feel perfect when we lost our baby. It didn't feel perfect when the day of our children's births were marked, as equally with grief for someone's greatest loss, as with joy for our greatest gain.

Saying that God's plan is perfect doesn't mean His plan is *easy*. Or *comfortable*. Or that it comes anywhere close to resembling the plan we made for ourselves. God's plan is perfect because it isn't about *me* at all. God's plan, when fulfilled in the lives of willing hearts, is all about HIM. When I look at my family, I see evidence of God's work, and it is beautiful.

Another lesson we learned through our journey is that in order to follow God's plan, we must remain very close to Him. Throughout the years, we have felt confusion over many decisions regarding our family. Should we pursue fertility treatments? If we pursue adoption instead, which agency should we use? Should we foster or adopt internationally? These were life-altering decisions, not just for us, but also for our future children. We wanted to be clear that the path we were taking was the way God wanted us to go. I learned that if I wanted to follow God, I had to pursue *Him*…not a child. I spent many, many hours just seeking to know Him better. In knowing Him, I began to recognize His voice. His voice led us to our children.

We also learned through this journey that God's timing is perfect. The day I found out that my unborn baby's heart had stopped beating was March 21, 2006. It was the first day of spring—a day that is supposed to signify renewal and life and hope was one of the darkest, deadest, most hopeless days of my life. I couldn't see past my pain, so I couldn't possibly have known what God knew.

God knew that seven and a half months later (only weeks after the due date of our baby) we would be bringing a baby home. My son was already in existence on March 21st. God knew my son still had a heartbeat, but that it just wasn't beating in my body.

God knew that exactly three years later on March 21st, I would write in my journal that a birthmother expecting a baby in less than a month had chosen us to adopt her son!

God knew that six years later on March 21st, we would accept the referral for a two-year-old little girl in China.

I know this is no coincidence! God has reminded us over and over that He does not make mistakes, and that He is never late.

After sharing this story with a friend, she encouraged me to look through the Bible, and see if there is something significant about 3:21. I was so excited to see what I could find; I couldn't wait until I got home to look! All I had was my phone, so I went to my Bible app and plugged in Genesis 3:21, Exodus 3:21, Leviticus 3:21, and so on. I went all the way through Revelation, and didn't feel anything was particularly significant about any 3:21.

Later that night, I pulled out my Bible and decided to look again. I remembered that 3:21 in Lamentations mentioned something about "hope," and wondered if that could be my verse. Lamentations 3:21 says, *"Yet this I call to mind and therefore I have hope:"* That's it. It's not even a whole sentence. It ends with a colon.

Could my life verse be only half a sentence—an unfinished thought? But the next few verses were already highlighted. Lamentations 3:22-26 say: "Because of the Lord's great love we are not consumed, for his compassions never fail. They are new every morning; great is your faithfulness. I say to myself, "The Lord is my portion; therefore I will wait for him." The Lord is good to those whose hope is in him, to the one who seeks him; it is good to wait quietly for the salvation of the Lord."

Through deeper study, I learned that the entire book of Lamentations through verse 3:20 was an expression of the people's overwhelming sense of loss that accompanied the destruction of Jerusalem and the temple. Chapter three, verse 21, however, is the spiritual high point of the entire book.

It marks a change in perspective. Just like Lamentations 3:21 was a turning point, March 21st was a turning point in my life. And just like I couldn't see the significance of that verse when I looked at it out of context, I couldn't see the significance of that day until years later when I saw the whole picture.

God has used the circumstances in my life to turn my eyes and my heart toward Him. When I took my focus off myself I was able to find Him...and to find hope.

Chapter 10

Anders and Paula's Story

Fear kept others from saying, "yes," and faith kept us from saying, "no"!

~

Our story began 22 years ago. My husband, Anders and I got married, bought a house, and had children...oh, no that was everyone else's story! That was our plan, but that didn't happen. We did get married and buy a house, but years went by with no children. It was the first time in our lives we realized some things were completely out of our control. No matter our plans and goals, or even our hard work, we could not make our dream of having children come true.

For five years we struggled, prayed, and spent a lot of money on fertility treatments, all with no success. A friend who had also struggled with infertility encouraged me with Bible verses, believing God would one day bless us with children. Verses like Psalm 37:4, which says to "delight yourself in the Lord, and he will give you the desires of your heart."

God also sent a very wise preacher, Rubin Smith who changed our lives forever. Rubin lead us to Romans 2:11, which explains that God shows no partiality. God wasn't punishing me for anything we did, or showing favor to other women instead of me. Rubin instructed me to find every woman in the Bible that struggled with infertility...Sarah, Hannah, Rachel, and Rebecca. Then he encouraged me to pray as God blessed them, He would bless us!

And He did!

Rewind. So the story goes like this: Emotionally drained after having a miscarriage, failed attempts to fix our fertility problems, and a fortune spent on those treatments, I had nothing to show but a broken heart and a feeling of being punished by God.

In August 1998 my grandmother, Margaret, passed away. There I was sad, frustrated and very disappointed, standing alone by her casket. As crazy as this sounds, I heard my grandmother say, plain as day, "Do not worry, Honey, your baby is on the way." A month later, my sister Donna, told me to call Bartow Family Resources immediately, she had heard of a young girl wanting to place her baby for adoption.

But, I didn't call, that was not my plan.

Days went by, and Anders and I decided we should call and at least hear about the situation. Soon we were meeting at the Center with the girl's stepmother and Becky Banks (who was the director of the Center at the time). It was a great meeting! Just a few weeks later we got a call: "You are going to have a baby girl in April 1999!"

The mother was a teenage girl who had been sent by her father to get an abortion, but by God's grace, because the Center was open...she chose life. How do you express your love and gratitude for such a gift? I tried to explain it in a letter to the best of my ability, but that didn't seem sufficient. We will forever be grateful that she chose life and gave us the *first* greatest gift ever!

As fear and uncertainty started arising with thoughts of adoption God spoke to me again. Not at a funeral this time, but in another strange place... the shower! He said, "Just like I told Mary, 'Fear not!'" I believe Jesus wants to give us much better gifts than we can ever plan. We only need to trust Him. As the Bible says, "Nothing will be impossible with God" (Luke 1:37) Our God is a loving, merciful Father. He does not punish us pointlessly or withhold blessings. Because of His grace, every good and perfect gift is from Him. We are His children; adopted into His family! And as a loving Father, as we seek to honor Him, He gives us our heart's desires.

As Anders and I "fought" over our daughter's name, I wanted Olivia. Anders wanted Jennifer (his favorite name). My grandmother, Margaret spoke again! This time from my dream. She was rocking our baby girl and said, "This baby's name is Mollie Margaret." I found out later my grandfather's mother's name was Mollie. Sharing the dream with Anders he said with good reason, "Well we do not argue with Margaret," and that was settled.

Although our daughter's birth mom did not want to meet us, the day after Mollie was born, circumstances changed. We believe God directed this meeting. It was definitely a gift to meet Mollie's birth mom, Catherine, and her family. We shared a special time together. I told them we would always raise Mollie to love her and that we would pray for her—and we have! I assured her that Mollie would know how much Catherine loved her to choose adoption. I also promised that Anders and I would raise Mollie in such a way that when they meet one day, she will be very proud of the woman she's become. And challenged her to use these years to become a woman that Mollie would be proud of as well. That time spent in the hospital was the most emotional two days of our lives!

Miracle #1: For this child we prayed. Mollie is the joy of our lives. Sixteen years later she is even more beautiful than the first day she was born—and she was the most beautiful baby ever born! Every night as Mollie got older we prayed for her birth mother...and she prayed for a baby brother.

Days passed into years with no other children. I continued to find encouragement praying my Bible verses; I often passed them out to other women struggling as well. At the age of 35, I was told I needed a hysterectomy. My doctor suggested if we wanted to try to have biological children we needed to try our last option, in vitro fertilization (IVF), before having the surgery.

Now at this point, we had done every infertility treatment available except IVF. I really struggled with what I viewed as "creating life" out of God's hands. But, as we researched about the procedure and spoke with our doctor, we quickly learned there is only so much they can do. It was completely in God's hands if life was created! I was also concerned how to manage any extra eggs, believing that all fertilized eggs were a human life. Well, God worked that out too, because the doctors were only able to get three eggs, and only three fertilized. So we used all three, but only one survived.

Here came miracle #2: A few weeks later we were pregnant! Not long after we found out we were having another precious girl. Anders was excited, but had to swallow hard, because he really thought we would have a boy!

No grandma Margaret this time…it was Anders who spoke to me. He said it was only fair she got a *Best* family name; my choice was Alberta Mabel or Sophie Marie. Without a second hesitation…Sophie it was. She is an amazing, beautiful, kind, and generous 12-year-old young lady.

Two beautiful girls, life was good! One grew in my tummy; one grew in my heart. Which when explaining this to Mollie as a 4-year-old, her response was, "how did your heart ever get that big?" Experiencing both a biological and adopted child, we can attest that there is not an ounce of difference in excitement or love. Mollie was our child from the moment we got the call five months before she was born. Mollie was gorgeous and Sophie was too. Sophie is the second greatest gift ever.

Fast-forward two years after Sophie was born; a hysterectomy was inevitable. We were so blessed to be the parents of two beautiful daughters. God answered our prayers! We loved sharing our story and continued passing out Bible verses to encourage others struggling with infertility. We truly believe if God puts the desire to be parents in a couple's heart, He will bless them with children! Six years pass by enjoying parenting 12-year-old, Mollie and Sophie who was eight. Anders was 48 and I was, well…let's just say I am younger than him! Our sights were set on college funds and retirement; our lives were full and complete!

Or so we thought!

Anders was serving on the board at the Resource Center and was active as chairman. I remember the moment vividly: We were sitting outside sharing about our day. I was telling Anders how I met a lady in her mid-40s, who desired desperately to have children but never did. Anders responded that I needed to have this woman call Cindy, because there was a pregnant lady looking for a family to adopt her baby. Then he said, "Hurry! She's about to deliver."

The Center had received calls from several people in the community about a homeless woman—obviously very pregnant—begging for money at Home Depot.

Apparently, this woman rode into our town on a bicycle and couldn't travel any further. Her plan was to have the baby at the hospital, leave him there, and be on her way. I called Cindy to tell her about the lady I met earlier that day. Cindy told me to call her because she had met with five couples and all of them said, "no." She had one more couple to ask. To my surprise, the woman I called was not interested in adoption either! As I called Cindy back, I surprised myself as the words came out of my mouth, "If no one else will, we will!"

The next morning Cindy called, she had been at the hospital the night before with the birth mother for what turned out to be "false labor." Cindy said, "The other couple said, "No", if you are serious about adopting this baby, I would like for you to meet her."

Whoa! Our hearts began beating fast now. The uncertainty of what we were doing became very real, yet felt so right. We went to meet her. The place was scary; she was shorter than me (which is really short), homeless, dirty, and very hungry. Cindy took her chicken to eat. I will never forget the picture of her eating a chicken leg, bone and all! She was feisty and full of personality.

We will be forever grateful to her and thankful the Center was able to minister to her right where she was. This was a picture of true love! Without hesitation, Cindy went to a "sketchy" motel to take her food, hygiene supplies, and clothes. She was Jesus' "hands and feet" in action. And this is just one example—there are so many situations like this that the staff and volunteers show Jesus' love to hurting individuals. It's inspiring to love people like Jesus does. The amazing staff and volunteers at the Center exemplify this day...and night!

Remember, Anders is approaching the big 5-0 at this point! If you are wondering about Anders, he responded, "I hope you know what you are doing. If we have another one don't expect me to change any diapers, and I'm only agreeing if it is a boy!" In sharing this with Mollie and Sophie, they were all in, happy to have either a little brother or sister. This all happened in only two weeks! Anders told us to wait to share this news. Given the circumstances that this birth mother was on cocaine, marijuana, and smoked a lot of cigarettes, he thought it may be a scam, or something could happen to the baby; plus we already knew what our friends and family would say!

Once again, I heard God say, "Do not fear, I have protected him in the womb." So, we decided not to tell anyone, which was extremely difficult! The girls and I were about to burst to tell someone. Finally, we twisted Anders arm to let us tell my sister, Donna. When I did she said, "You better really think about this." The day the birth mother had a doctor's appointment my sister drove up to our house bringing a balloon she had discovered. It was half-deflated and leaning against our gate; it was a blue 3-foot teddy bear balloon that said, "It's a boy!" We live in the middle of nowhere! No one knows where we live but God, and He sends us a balloon just a few hours before Cindy called and said, "It's definitely a boy!" Wow! From early years of feeling neglected or punished to being showered and thrilled by God's love and presence.

It is so important to listen to God (and your husband). While everyone means well and believes they are giving advice for our good, we only have One to listen and answer to. This woman, Cheyenne, gave this amazing gift! In the best way she could in her circumstance, she protected and valued his life. Had we told our family and friends and taken their advice of saying, "no" we would have missed out on the third greatest gift ever.

We welcomed an 8 pounds, 14 ounces beautiful *and* healthy, baby boy to our family. We used a mix of family names for him, his first name is after my father, Jack, and his middle name is Anders. Jackson tested positive for cocaine and marijuana. The doctor said he should have a low birth weight, could be crying for weeks, and would not cuddle. But again, God is faithful! Jackson did not cry often and was a sweet, cuddler. The pediatrician could not believe it. Fear kept others from saying, "yes," and faith kept us from saying, "no"! He is miracle #3.

After a few days of recovery, Jackson's birth mother, a hero of ours was on her way and left our lives as quickly as she entered. Cindy said she seemed happy as she peddled away on her new bike.

For this child we prayed…and forgot. Anders got his boy, Mollie and Sophie got their baby brother and I am gifted to be their mother! God answers prayer. Period. Maybe twelve years later than we thought, but the gift of Jackson couldn't be any better or more perfect timing.

Three awesome miracles! Two great diaper changers, and one crazy, fun, active, beautiful baby boy! Jackson is now four, engaged in everything, he is intelligent like his daddy and he looks just like me. Anders says we did not know we wanted another baby until we got one. Now our lives are complete (we are quite certain!). Our surprise miracle is an amazing, brilliant, happy and full of life kid from sun up until *way* past sun down. We would not change a thing! This was the song God gave me when we had his dedication at our church.

Out of the blue one day,
You came to us this way.
An unexpected surprise, an addition to our lives,
What God has in store is always so much more.
We trusted Him, spoke no fear and walked through the door.

'Cause we don't know what we've done to deserve this little one,
Thank you God for this gift our son,
We don't know what to say, all we know to do
Is love him and give him back to you.

Some things may seem strange, some called us insane,
What better place to be than doing God's will.
All things work for good, when we trust Him like we should
God has a plan for you our little man.

God has a purpose and a plan! Trust Him it is always better than you can imagine. We thank God that I could not get pregnant, and we thank God I did! We will be forever grateful for Bartow Family Resources and their doors being open! Our community is a better place because of their love and service.

(Thread with Chapter Fifteen: Mollie's Story)

Chapter 11

Jeff and Kelley's Story

*God already knew the baby inside the birth mom's womb. God knew
this baby was not a mistake. He was not a problem. He was not a
burden. And he was not an inconvenience. This pregnancy was not
an accident. It was not a punishment. This baby was a miracle.*

⁓

O ur story begins with a marriage of two best friends. Jeff and I were
married in the church I grew up in on October 9, 1993. I was a special
needs teacher working on a graduate degree and Jeff was a pharmaceuti-
cal sales representative. Everything was wonderful…except our struggle to
have children.

In 1999, we sought help from a fertility specialist. The doctors discovered that I had a pretty significant case of endometriosis. With the help of
surgery, the doctors were able to remove it. We were excited once again
that since we "found" the reason of infertility, soon we would get pregnant
with our first child.

But that didn't happen. Over the next months, after blood work, medication, tests, probes, temperature charts, and visits to the doctor, no cause
of our infertility was found! According to medical statistics, 2% of the population struggling with infertility falls into an "unknown" category. And
that is where Jeff and I were placed.

Doctors didn't give up on us and believed strongly we could have
children—it was just a matter of time. They gave us many options. The
first was the least invasive and most inexpensive. So with anticipation we

tried insemination (IUI). After two unsuccessful attempts, the doctors told us to give it one more try since it was common to try an IUI three times before moving on to another option.

On the day before our third attempt, couples from our church and our pastor gathered with us to pray. I remember the exact words of that prayer. Dr. Davidson prayed to God about the desires of our heart to care for a child and asked him to bless us with a baby. Within two weeks we knew that our third attempt was unsuccessful.

The next week, Becky Banks from the Cartersville Pregnancy Care Center told us that a couple had come into the pregnancy center for a pregnancy test. The test was positive and the mom was confused as to what to do. She was considering abortion, but was also considering keeping the baby. The counselors from the center talked to her about the options available to her. They also told her there were many families unable to have children, waiting to adopt. As this woman realized these difficult circumstances were not the baby's fault, she made the decision to carry to term. And in learning about her options, she decided she wanted to choose adoption.

It says in Psalm 139:13-16, "for you created me in your inmost being; you knit me together in my mother's womb. I praise you because you are fearfully and wonderfully made; your works are wonderful, I know that full well. My frame was not hidden from you when I was made in the secret place. When I was woven together in the depths of the Earth, your eyes saw my unformed body."

God already knew the baby inside the birth mom's womb. God knew this baby was not a mistake. He was not a problem. He was not a burden. And he was not an inconvenience. This pregnancy was not an accident. It was not a punishment. This baby was a miracle.

Shortly after this couple's decision, the staff at the pregnancy center prayed for this little child. They asked God to reveal who should meet with the parents about the possibility of adopting their baby. The parents needed to know quickly there were loving parents that were willing to meet with them and discuss adopting their child. The staff felt in their hearts that we would be one of the couples that would meet with the parents. Becky Banks, who was director of the center at the time, said as the staff prayed God kept bringing us to their minds.

Completely nervous, we met with the birth mother and the birth father. It was a wonderful meeting! During our meeting, the birth mother said that we were just what she was hoping for. She did not want to interview any other couples. She wanted us to be the ones to adopt her baby. WOW!

This was going to be an open adoption. We would participate in the prenatal and perinatal support. I met with the birth mom to decide how much I would be involved. The mom shared with me about where they were in life and how their environment wouldn't be a good one for raising a child. After much discussion, she decided I was to be involved in every appointment. So, I picked her up for every doctor's visit. I saw every ultrasound picture. We found out together that it was a baby boy. With this news, Jeff was excited...ready to get out his worn mitt for some father-son baseball in the front yard!

Within our conversations, we discovered how much the Lord was present in this whole process. Amazingly, we found out that the birth mom was as far along in her pregnancy as I would have been if the last insemination had worked. You see, the night that our pastor prayed for us, he prayed that God would give us a baby. He never mentioned pregnancy in the prayer. God heard our wants during that prayer and gave us exactly what we prayed for. That continues to give me chills every time I think of it. This was miraculous!

God and two human beings acted in love and gave us the most beautiful and perfect gift, the gift of their son. John 3:16 says "For God so loved the world that he gave us his one and only son that who-so-ever believes in him should not perish but have everlasting life." In part, I can understand what a painful act of love that was, as this couple gave up their precious son.

Time for delivery! I got to be right there in the delivery room. Right after the C-section, I was handed our newborn son. The birth mom chose to see and hold him. He was absolutely beautiful. He had a head of blonde hair and little rosebud lips. Honestly, the cutest newborn that I had ever seen. We named him, Kyle Patrick.

When you study the Scripture, it becomes clear that we are all adopted. In Ephesians 1:11, it says, "In him, we were also chosen having been predestined according to the plan of him who works everything in conformity with the purpose of his will." Kyle was not given up. Kyle was chosen, just like God has chosen us to be Christians. Our Lord and Savior has adopted us! How perfectly our adoption of Kyle showed God's love for His children!

When Kyle was 8-months old, we made the decision to try more options at the Reproductive Specialist. Jeff felt we were supposed to try to have biologically children too. We decided to skip straight to in vitro fertilization, since it had the greatest success rate. It worked! In fact, it worked so well I found out we were pregnant with twins. Kyle was going to be the big brother!

As we prepared for more children, we discovered that both babies were boys. The pregnancy went well. I went to my routine doctor visits with my Obstetrician. At 31 weeks, I went to a doctor's visit for an ultrasound. The doctor could find one strong heartbeat, but only faintly heard the second. To be safe, he decided to send me to the hospital to be sure everything was fine. The nurse put a monitor on my belly and listened for the heartbeats.

A little while later, a high-risk pregnancy doctor came in to check on the babies. Since I was expecting twins, I was considered high-risk. The perinatologist looked at the monitor while he was listening for heartbeats. After a couple of minutes, the doctor told me "Baby A" no longer had a heartbeat. Jeff and I were devastated. It was a terribly emotional time.

We said 'good bye' to Samuel Jeffrey before welcoming him to our home. No one prepares for the news of losing a child. The perinatologist and obstetrician decided to admit me to the hospital for a night of monitoring. If everything was good we could go home the next day.

As I lay in the bed that night, "Baby B's" heart rate declined. The first time it happened, the nurse was able to help the baby move around and get his heart rate back up. The second time it happened, my obstetrician was called. He stayed at the hospital to closely watch our little one. When it happened a third time, the doctor decided I had to deliver immediately!

After an emergency C-section, I gave birth at 31 weeks of pregnancy. Baby Sam was delivered first to allow more room for the delivery of our healthy son. We welcomed, Jackson Thomas weighing a robust 3 pounds, 9 ounces!

On October 3, 2001 at 2:37 am, Jack came into the world with a mission and purpose to fulfill on earth. Our Sam came into the world with his purpose fulfilled. Sam was a hero; he saved his twin brother's life by losing his own. If I had not been on the monitor that evening, it was a fact that both babies would have died. Sam was *my* hero and was sitting with the Hero of all heroes, Jesus Christ. I long to hold him. I can't wait to embrace my son one day in Heaven. Since Jack was so early and so tiny, he was released from the NICU after five weeks. Our family of four began.

Kyle was a quiet baby and toddler. He didn't cry or show much emotion. He was just happy and content. Jack, however, had colic. He didn't sleep well, didn't like to be swaddled, and was a typical, high-maintenance, preemie. As he grew Jack was a beautiful toddler, known for his adorable chunky cheeks!

Life was busy, but fun. And I loved my time with my boys. I loved watching them discover faces, lights, and objects. I loved watching them walk in the grass for the first time, play in the sprinkler, and chase butterflies. Life was good, but I had one thing that I could not forget in my mind.

When we did in vitro fertilization with Jack and Sam, we had four embryos left that were frozen. In vitro has many ethical and moral implications that we had to work through, and I was not willing to just let them perish. We believed life began at conception, so these embryos were in fact children waiting to be born. We needed to make a decision about them.

Do you give them to couples that are unable to have children? Do you try in vitro fertilization again? Do you let them die? It was a hard decision that we prayed about it for a long time. There is no guarantee as to whether you will get pregnant or not. There is no guarantee that the babies will live through the thawing process. Twenty-one months after Jack was born, our decision was to try in vitro for a second time.

With the help from a Reproductive Specialist, we found that two embryos were still viable, and one only had ¼ of the necessary cells, after going through the thawing process. So, we choose the two healthy embryos, as well as the one that was not deemed "viable." I had to know they were all given the chance for life.

Within weeks, we were blessed with the news that we were pregnant again with twins. We saw a perinatalogist quickly in our pregnancy. At 20 weeks, I was put on bed rest. This time…we were having a boy and a girl! At 28 weeks of pregnancy, my body went into labor.

I was rushed to the hospital. The doctors met us there and I delivered two preemie babies at 28 weeks gestation. Joshua Allen was born weighing a whopping 2 pounds, 11 ounces and Layne Elizabeth weighed just 2 pounds. Both were released from the NICU after 7 ½ weeks. Josh came home weighing 4 pounds and Layne came home weighing 3 pounds, 11 ounces. But, the six of us were snuggly at home!

We had a lot of difficulty having children of our own. Half joking, I tell everyone that I was a bad "incubator." I know that every child in our family has an amazing story, so I don't regret our decision, but at times, I question whether God intended for me to give birth to children.

From a couple that struggled with infertility, to a couple with four children is nothing short of miraculous! Our journey was long and hard but it was worth every minute, the hands of God guided every prayer and step. We learned how to truly depend on our Father. We learned how He answers prayers. We learned that when we cry, He also cries. We learned that when we rejoice, He rejoices with us. It says in Psalm 37:4, "Delight yourself in the Lord and he will give you the desires of your heart." God gave us our desires, not in the way we imagined it would happen, but in the perfect way that would change our lives forever.

(Thread with Chapter Sixteen: Kyle's Story)

Chapter 12

Doug and Sarah's Story

Happy as a family of four, preparing to answer God's call was both uncharted territory and uncomfortable! But, we trusted God's direction.

~

"Belisle, party of five." We hadn't planned it that way. Doug and I moved from Texas to Georgia in 2007 with our two children. Doug was the new associate pastor at Cartersville First Baptist Church. We had a three-year-old son, Jack, and a 9-month old daughter, Grace. Honestly, we were very satisfied with our "perfect" family of four. Having children worked out just as we had planned and since we had a boy and a girl, we were complete. At least that's what we thought.

October 2009: Doug attended a conference in Atlanta. After hearing a speaker share God's call to Christians to adopt, his heart was burdened. One message was centered on Isaiah 1:17, God's command to care for the widows and orphans. The speaker explained that although not every Christian is called to adopt, we are all commanded to pray for orphans and pray for God to reveal our part in the adoption process.

When Doug got home, he asked me to pray with him about God's direction for us to possibly begin our own adoption journey. I was totally unnerved by the thought. So, we both prayed for a time. Soon we came to the decision that we should take a step of faith. We felt called to adopt.

As we prayed we also realized there are many other couples that could adopt, even feel called to adopt, but don't because of fears or threatened comforts. Happy as a family of four, preparing to answer God's call was both uncharted territory and uncomfortable! But, we trusted God's direction. We started praying about how, when, where, and who? We felt compelled to adopt cross culturally, and we were to adopt a boy. Jack helped us name him Judah, which means, "Praise." We also loved the Bible verse in 2 Chronicles 14:4 that says, "He commanded *Judah* to seek the LORD, the God of their ancestors, to obey His laws and commands." So, we waited for our Judah.

February 2010: Doug and I met with the director of the Bartow Family Resources. We talked about submitting our profile to the attorney they use when connecting birth moms with adoptive families. During our meeting we were told we couldn't choose gender or race, so we felt this was a closed door. But the director encouraged me to create a "profile" anyway and see what happened. It snowed that day; in faith we created a snowman family of our future family of five. Some of the neighbors thought that the Judah snowman meant we were getting a dog. Apparently, our snowman making skills were not very good!

Right after our meeting I started working on our profile.

July 2010: While visiting my parents in Texas, we visited an adoption agency, but left knowing the agency was not a good match. Driving home we decided to investigate Bethany Christian Services, an amazing agency that was highlighted at the conference that first sparked Doug's heart for adoption. We went to a meeting and decided to submit our profile. But for some reason, I never finished sending in our information.

November 2010: Thanksgiving week arrived and my plan was to finish the paperwork and get our Bethany Agency profile mailed. But, again I just couldn't get it done. If you know me, you would know this had to be supernatural, because I am a skilled organizer.

On November 29th at 8:45 pm the phone rang…it was Cindy, the director from Bartow Family Resources. Doug answered the phone to the question: "Are you still interested in adoption?" He said "yes", and she said that she thought that she had found *our Judah.*

Doug got off the phone and told me the Cindy said that a bi-racial boy was due in March and wanted to know if we were interested. I was calm until he said the baby was due in *March*. Two weeks earlier, Jack's Sunday school teacher told me that Jack was talking about his baby brother Judah. She wondered if we were expecting or adopting. I explained we were adopting, but we didn't know when. She continued to explain that Jack said his dad was bringing home his baby brother in *March*. What! We were both equally amazed and shaken! (Jack became a Christian in October, so we know that he and the Lord had close communication). We decided to meet the birth mother a week later.

December 2010: At an annual Ladies Christmas Dinner, which benefited the pregnancy center, Cindy told me the birth mom was already telling people that a local pastor was adopting her baby—even though we hadn't met yet!

We met the birth mom that Friday and had a wonderful meeting. As we prayed over the next weekend, we asked God to confirm this was our child or quickly close the door. God gave us confirmation and excitement.

When Cindy was talking to the birth mom after our meeting, she wanted to know if we had already picked out a name. Cindy told her yes, and the mom said, "Oh, well, I wanted to see if they would consider naming him a name that starts with the letter, J."

Then Cindy excitedly shared with her that we chose the name, Judah. The birth mom said, "Do they have a middle name picked out yet?" Cindy said, "No." The birth-mom replied, "Well, if it starts with the letter L, then I have made my decision. They are clearly the ones that are supposed to have my baby."

Upon hearing this, we were even more amazed. When we asked Jack what his brother's middle initial should be, he said (with an attitude of "duh"), the letter, L." His initials would be JLB. Jack acted as if we were supposed to already know that!

January 2011: Doug and I were invited to go to the doctor with the birth mom! We heard Judah's heartbeat. So cool! During one of the appointments, the midwife asked the birth mom who was going to cut the umbilical cord. She looked at Doug and said, "Ya wanna?" and he said, "Sure!" Over the next couple months we shared some really special meetings with the birth mom.

March 2011: On March 3rd, we received a call letting us know that the birth mom would be delivering in the next two days. The next day, at 8:30 am in the morning, we got the call that she would be delivering *that* afternoon. They asked us to be at the hospital at 10:30 am to finish laboring with her. Wow!

I labored with her until 1:45 pm. When instruments were coming out and people were gloving up, I went to the lobby and got Doug. As she finished laboring, Doug waited in the corner of the room!

Around 2 pm she started pushing. Twelve minutes later, we welcomed Judah into our family. Doug came out from "time out" as the nurses joked, and cut the cord. Judah Lucas was 8 pounds, 12 ounces and 20.5 inches long.

While in the hospital, we had some very special times with the birth mom. We took some pictures with her and her family. My dad led her in an unforgettable prayer time after she signed the surrender papers.

When Judah was just 24 hours old, we took him *home*. Doug announced our adoption in church the following Sunday. Our church family started clapping and cheering. It was so special!

Two months passed and it was time to go to court to finalize Judah's adoption. The day had come for us to make this entire process officially complete. Doug and I had been through the paperwork, home study, and physicals; and now we were going to petition the court to grant us the privilege to adopt this sweet child as our own!

On June 1st, 2011 we celebrated Judah's "Gotcha Day," the day he officially became apart of our family. Judah Lucas was given a new last name. Now, he will always have that name. The amazing thing about adoption "being official" is on Judah's birth certificate, it says that Doug and I are his parents; nothing different than if I had birthed him. Judah is ours forever. What a beautiful picture of our own salvation experience. God sought us out and CHOSE us as His own, so that through Jesus, and the Spirit of adoption, we might be called the sons and daughters of God.

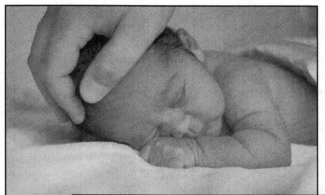

Stories from Adopted Children

I was chosen.
I was wanted.
I was cherished.
I grew in their hearts.
I was the missing piece.
I was loved.
I was ADOPTED.

Chapter 13

Amy Grace's Story

I realize that I am fully complete through Christ Jesus,
a new creation, lacking nothing. He has given me eyes
that are open to realize that I am a child of destiny.

~

My parents Danny and Kathy were very proactive in adoption. They knew many families who had adopted and they desired to adopt. For eight years my parents' names were listed on the Department of Family and Children Services adoption approved list while they anticipated adopting a child. During this time they experienced a failed adoption. Before DFCS could be the avenue to grow their family, they were able to have a private adoption through a friend of the family.

First, they adopted my brother and then had a second failed adoption attempt. Finally, four years later they received a phone call from DFCS stating that they had a baby. My parents had recently moved and DFCS office randomly pulled their name from the top of a large stack of papers. Random for DFCS, but perfectly orchestrated by God.

DFCS called my parents and mentioned that they had the "Gerber Baby." So my parents went to the foster home and met a sweet lady named Miss Dottie. Dottie was known to foster children with special needs. In her home at that time she had a 4-year old autistic boy and the "Gerber Baby," a beautiful newborn baby girl…also known as *me*. DFCS sought to place me in a home that had an older sibling, because my eyes would light up every time I saw Miss Dottie's other foster child. In February 1985, my parents welcomed me home.

Growing up my parents always emphasized that I was adopted first in God's family and second in their family. My mother read a book on adoption nightly and it was always my favorite. This was an open story in our house, and it was never a secret. My parents were honest about the circumstances of our adoption. They prepared my brother and me by studying scripture with us about adoption, which helped teach us we were part of God's perfect plan.

My earliest memories are filled with lots of love, encouragement, and lots of fun. My parents even lead us in Bible devotionals at an early age. My mama played the piano and taught me how to sing. Even though my pitch was less than perfect, she never gave up! My daddy believed in me and taught me about the Bible. What impacted me the most about my parents was they didn't just talk the talk; they walked the walk. My teachers in school would always mention that I was the light of their classroom.

One of my fondest memories is watching the video of my baptism. Growing up in a glass house, given that my daddy was a minister, I had been to revival across the states of Georgia and South Carolina at least 500 times before age four.

At a very young age of five, I confessed my faith in Jesus Christ. I loved Jesus and knew Jesus loved me. In October 1989 my daddy was preparing to baptize me. The baptismal sat above the choir loft between the giant organ pipes. As my daddy led the prayer, he began to baptize me. During this experience I must have thought I was drowning because both of my feet flew up to the sky. I proceeded to kick water with my arms and legs all over the back row of the choir. This is something that our family still laughs about to this day. Those poor choir members on the back row!

Being a strong-willed child, I typically fought family devotionals, but daddy won the battle each and every time! Firm foundations were built early on, and I came to know the love of God at a very early age. When I was growing up, and even to this day, people compliment how much I look like my mama and/or how much I look like my daddy.

While those compliments are incredibly touching now, there was a time in my adolescence that these uninformed statements would become twisted by the enemy and rob me of my joy. The enemy constantly tried to deceive me by telling me I could never be as good as them. Since I was not their biological child.

So the area of acceptance became something that stunted my spiritual development. The enemy lied to me and told me I would never be enough. What a big, fat, liar! I knew the truth from scripture that says, "Greater is He that is in me than he that is in the world." Now looking back I realize that I am fully complete through Christ Jesus, a new creation, lacking nothing. He has given me eyes that are open to realize that I am a child of destiny. My story is just a tiny part of His greater story, and He is using my life to fulfill His Kingdom purposes.

If I could tell my birth mother one thing it would be thank you for fulfilling God's plan for your life by sacrificing your relationship with me. Because of your decision and preservation of my life, I now have a deeper understanding of sacrificial love. Her decision helped to form deep within me God's unwavering grace. It also inspires me to tell about the wonderful things Jesus has done for me. I would want her to know how much I love her and pray for her to be a believer, to live a fulfilled life. I would also want her to know that she made the best decision for me!

Throughout my years, when I listened to Satan's lies, I have struggled with adoption and acceptance. But those struggles were rooted in lies. If you are an adopted child, I want you to hear what I learned, the truth of adoption—*Before the world was ever formed, God knew you. God knew how many hairs were on your head, even where you should live. Nothing catches God by surprise! You were fearfully and wonderfully made. God placed you with the exact parents He wants you to have for your good. God chose you. And so did your parents. You are a gift!*

One day my mom told me the story about when my brother asked why God allowed his birth mother to get pregnant? My mom said, "God allows permissive will and God took the birth mother's sorrow and turned it to *our* joy." There are many occasions where joy and sorrow meet. Adoption is normally such an occasion. As God works all things for our good and His glory, He turns these occasions into his perfect will.

My mother is my best friend and my daddy is my hero. They have always been there for me and loved me. I do wish I could re-live four years of my adolescence! If I could, I would have chosen to be obedient, walk in truth, and not be as rebellious! Simply put, I wouldn't have listened to the lies of the deceiver, who was only out for my harm. My life could have turned out very differently if I had continued believing those lies; instead I chose to believe truth.

Bartow Family Resources walked alongside me after high school when I sought counsel from them. Many years later, I still have deep friendships with them and stay involved through the connection we have with our church's involvement in the ministry. They meant so much to me in helping me cling to truth.

During that time of rebellion, I am so thankful to my parents for trusting the Holy Spirit to work internally and intentionally within me. They are fervent prayer warriors, gifted musicians, and love the Lord with all their hearts, minds, souls, and strength. Psalm 34:10 states, "Those that seek the Lord shall not lack any good thing." My parents are proof of this. Even through difficulties, God provides for our every need.

My brother, Wesley and I were very close as we grew up and continue that relationship now. We always recognized that we were siblings, even if people would question if we were biologically family or not. I cannot tell you how many times people would raise the question, is he your real brother? Yes, he is my *real* brother!

Wesley and I loved exploring the woods near our house, riding bicycles all over the neighborhood, and playing Super Mario Brothers on the Nintendo. I have many happy memories growing up because of him. I am proud of my brother and I know he is proud of me.

God is certainly good…I am now married to my wonderful husband, Jeromy, and the mother of two beautiful girls. On Sundays I serve in the Children's ministry teaching 3rd grade girls and sing in the worship choir. After my first year teaching high school, I was chosen as the school's New Teacher of the Year. Shortly after I switched to work with children at the elementary school, and I have been there ever since! In the spring of 2014, I was inducted in Delta Kappa Gamma International for key women educators. In the 2014-2015 school year I was surprised to be chosen as the teacher of the year for my school and then I was chosen as one of three finalists for the school district!

Currently, I am pursuing my Masters in Education. Teaching in the public school for the past six years has opened my eyes to the breakdown of the American home. Many of our students live in poverty that goes unnoticed. My job gives me an opportunity to invest in something greater than myself. My vocation is my mission field, and I am using every tool God has given me to minister to children and families. I share my accomplishments to showcase all the God has done. They were not achieved in my own power. No, they are because my dear birth mother gave me the gift of my parents, who introduced me to the God that has the power to do such incredible work through me! To whom much is given, much is required.

In January of 2015, I began a blog about Christ's impact on my life. The Holy Spirit is working through my life as I write. Through my blog I am stepping out in faith and allowing Him to use my words to meet a lost world. And by sharing my life, other people are given an opportunity to see what it is like to live a life fulfilled in Christ. He calls each of us to fulfill the purposes He has already planned for our lives. My story is a story rooted in His forgiveness, unfathomable grace, redemption, mercy, and peace. I hope you learn to experience this same joy as you find your fulfillment in Christ!

Chapter 14

Matthew's Story

Being adopted is both a blessing and opportunity
from God to have a second chance.

~

I was most likely going to be aborted like several other siblings before me, but through God's sovereignty my birth mother was incarcerated instead. Simply, God said I was to live and breathe on this earth, and so I was. And God said who my parents would be, and led them to me. My mom (not birth mother) was there through labor and delivery and even got to cut my cord. She and my dad weren't looking to adopt, their kids were about grown, but God had different plans for them.

My birth mother left me several times with my mom, because at that time my mom was the Director of the Resource Center. She would not come back for several weeks at a time. DFCS got involved and after many months trying to help my birth mother decided to terminate her rights, they told my mom she could adopt me or put me in the foster care system. As I was already a part of their family, my mom and dad (and super loving sisters) could not fathom that. So on September 5, 1995 I officially became a Banks.

Being adopted is both a blessing and opportunity from God to have a second chance. Being a Banks means I was given an opportunity to receive love and learn to give love. It means God gave me an amazing story to share. The special bond with my God-given family is immeasurable, and to be perfectly accepted into my family loved and provided for is inspiring.

But, most importantly, being gifted a family who truly loves God. That is the greatest gift of adoption.

And because of this great gift, being adopted has presented a testimony I can share with others about how God has miraculously saved my life from true darkness (both physically and spiritually) for His purpose. At times I think about what life would have been like if I had been raised in my biological family, a family with no Christian background...where would I be now?

God has blessed me so much in my life. I'm more than just lucky to have a family who not only fought for my life when I was too small to have a voice, but also have worked hard to provide for me, care for me, and show me God's love! Words and sentences are pretty hard to sum up how much love, affection and happiness I have toward God. For my Loving Father has created me to be a Banks.

(Thread with Chapter Six)

Chapter 15

Mollie's Story

*Growing up an adopted child was not difficult, and then
again, was different. I learned I was adopted at such a
young age it has always been part of who I am.*

~

My name is Mollie, I am 16 years old, and my mother and father, Anders and Paula, adopted me as a baby. My parents have told me since before I could understand that I was adopted. Anytime we talked about adoption, I was told what a wonderful gift I was and how much my birth mother loved me to give me this life.

So I have grown up thinking there was something very special about adoption. And as I have gotten older that has only become more and more true for me. There is something very special about knowing that your birth mother loved you enough to pick the perfect family for you when she didn't think she would be enough. My family is a great supporter of adoption and always will be.

My story started about 17 years ago when my biological mom got pregnant with me at the age of 16. I have been told that her stepmother took her to Bartow Family Resources, known then as The Crisis Pregnancy Center, to talk about their options. I have also been told they were considering abortion, but hoped for another option. Fortunately, there was someone at the Center to listen and give advice that encouraged them to choose an option that gave me life!

Growing up an adopted child was not difficult, and then again, was different. I learned I was adopted at such a young age it has always been part of who I am. I have been blessed with the best parents I could have hoped for and a family that surrounds and supports me. They are the best people possible; I could not have hoped for anything better. We still fight and argue and stand up for each other. We are a normal family.

However in some ways I have always felt like something was sort of "missing." By that I mean I've often wondered about how someone I have never met could be so special to me. Even though I do not know her right now, my biological mom will always hold a special place in my heart, no matter what the future holds. As I have gotten older, I understand my parents will always be my parents. They do not consider me any differently than their biological child.

Meeting my biological family has always been important to me; one day I hope to meet all of them. As I have gotten older my mother and father have begun opening doors for me.

Last year because of a school project my parents gave me the clothes my biological mom bought for me to wear home from the hospital. They also gave me a framed drawing of a butterfly she had done for me. Looking at that drawing and outfit made me wonder even more. And I am so eager to know more!

My mom recently arranged for me to meet my biological step great-grandmother—though she wasn't my biological grandmother she knew my biological family well. As we visited I learned more about my biological family in one day than I have known in 16 years. Even though I have waited so long to find these things out I didn't know what to do or even really what questions to ask when the time came. Fortunately, she just talked and talked, which was a relief and allowed me to get to know her.

When people find out you are adopted they often have questions, which I have always been comfortable answering. My parents arranging for me to meet a family member of my biological family was very special to me. They have always answered questions for me, but now I was getting answers to questions they didn't even know! After finding information about my biological mom I found myself more interested than ever in what we have in common or the things that she may be curious to learn about me. I wonder if she ever thinks about me, or if she met me today she would be proud of the young lady I have become.

Hopefully, one day in the future I will get to meet her. And my hope is to have a relationship with her. As for now the information and friendship I have gained has made me feel as if I have learned something new about myself. My parents have made me who I am today and I am forever grateful. I've learned it's only natural to wonder about the person who gave birth to me and allowed me to be who I am today.

I am so thankful for Bartow Family Resources because without them I wouldn't have the privilege to live the life that I do. To me adoption is the perfect answer to a crisis pregnancy and a family desiring a child. It has opened up so many doors for me in my life. I pray the center stays in our county for years and years in the future so they can continue to bless the people of our community. They have blessed my life and so many with the work they do.

(Thread with Chapter Ten)

Chapter 16

Kyle's Story

*Every adopted child should feel optimistic
about the life they have been given.*

~

I have known I was adopted since the very beginning of my life. Though my understanding of what that meant took awhile longer. Every night before bed, my mom would ask me *who* was her "dream come true." I would say I was. God's love for us is equal, no matter what. And we are adopted into His family. My rich Christian background and belonging to a great church, I realize what a wonderful family in Christ I have.

Sure, there were some fears while growing up. Many of my fears, however, had more to do with my hearing disability and "growing pains" then to do with adoption. I'm a teenager now, and I have faith that I will make it in life with strength from Christ, family, and friends. My "small" fears are being overcome with the encouragement of my church and family.

My greatest memory growing up was going to my grandmother's condo in Saint Simons Island, GA. We had so much fun each year; since we went so many times, we knew just about everything there is to know about the island. Going there always filled me with comfort. My grandparents sold the condo last year, after owning it for 20 years. I was lucky to have those experiences.

In my childhood I have had some of the brightest moments a kid could have. Especially, the awesome nickname given to me by my dad, "Pumpkin."

My parents took me three years in a row to a really cool Christian camp called Pine Cove in Texas. I learned so much about God there, and of course, I got to be my crazy self! Making friends was easy at camp.

My mom and dad have always tried to help me understand how special I am. On my fourteenth birthday, I went to a concert for Newsboys, Jamie Grace, Third Day, and other Christian musicians. My mom kept this a secret for a whole year! It meant a lot to me. I'm fifteen now, so I guess I'm legally able to drive! Just hoping I pass my learner's test.

If I could tell my birth mom something it would be that she made the right decision to put me up for adoption. With the help of the Center, she was given adoption as an option, and thankfully, she didn't choose to abort me. I thank God every day for my life, and for my parents and their dedication to teach me through life's challenges. Like me, every adopted child should feel optimistic about the life they have been given. They should cherish every moment they have, tomorrow isn't promised. As God protected my life, He is planning each step into my future.

My family is so fun to be around. Sure, like most families, we fight and argue at times. I'll admit, I've even hit my brothers, but if anyone tries to hurt them they are my family to protect (especially, my sister!). I love the jokes my dad makes about his running shoes. I love the way my mom plans things out—it may be annoying—but we wouldn't get anywhere if she didn't! I love my family!

God has spoken to me once in my 15 years of life. It was at a youth trip from church. All He said was "In time, it will be done." I am yet to find out what it completely means, but I know it means I have a great future ahead in His divine plan. My favorite Bible verse is 1 Corinthians 16:13, "Be watchful, stand firm in the faith, act like men, be strong." It means to stay strong no matter what, be respectful of others, and always pay attention to God's plan. God has plans for me and I can't wait to find out what they are.

(Thread with Chapter Eleven)

Chapter 17

Amy's Story

*I look back now and can see little places along the way that
God tried to reach out to me—the One trying to heal my
heart—but I was too busy being wounded to listen.*

~

The story starts before I was born. It starts with a teenage girl and her boyfriend. She got pregnant and was faced with a decision to abort her baby. Through counseling with a pastor at her church she made the decision not to have an abortion, but instead to give the baby up for adoption. During this time there was another couple that had tried to have a baby but they could not conceive. Having a child was their dream so they began the long and expensive process of adoption.

Enter me. My birthmother (we will call her Sue) gave birth to me on March 23, 1980 and named me Samantha. I was born with pneumonia. My precious birthmother and her family did not want me to be alone in the hospital while I was recovering, so they stayed with me for a week. Could you imagine trying to hold your baby long enough to make up for a lifetime in seven days? That is true love. Once I was ready to be released, my birthmother signed the adoption papers and walked out of my life.

What a fabulous gift she gave my adopted family and me. She made a courageous decision and gave me life. I will forever be grateful. And I am especially thankful that she chose *my* parents. My mom and dad are amazing people. They knew from the moment that they saw me that I was meant to be theirs. God knit our family together supernaturally and chose them for me, and me for them before the foundation of the world. I was theirs and they loved me as wholeheartedly as any biological child.

Seriously, I can't imagine life without a love as strong as theirs supporting me. I would have never made it. My parents raised me to know I was miraculously adopted, and they always, always, always told me how much I was loved. However, as we each have our own stories of struggles and victories, this is *my* story.

Perhaps because of my adoption, I was very sensitive to finding my identity—how and where I belonged. Though many young people struggle with fitting in, I let my struggles define me. I learned it was not until I realized my true identity that I could truly live.

Growing up I always knew I was different. I was adopted into a family with a strong Hispanic heritage. Although my aunts and uncles loved me, I never felt like I fit since I didn't look like my family. I felt like the odd one in the crowd. Growing up it was funny because I was tall and my dad was tall, so there were times people would make a comment about me being "tall like my dad." Sometimes I would feel pride that I was being associated with him and my family. But other days it would sting reminding me that it was "impossible" to look like my dad since I wasn't his biologically!

As kids often do, I was told hurtful things in an angry attempt to hurt me about how I didn't really belong ...and as one classmate put it, "it was no surprise your birthmother threw you away." The saying goes, "It takes ten nice things to replace one hurtful word." I wholeheartedly believed these hurtful words over any encouragement in my life. And the hurt defined me.

Oh, it may be helpful to note that during Elementary School and Middle School I had a few other defining issues; my allergies would get to be so bad in the spring I couldn't do outdoor activities with the other kids, so I became known as the book nerd; I not only had buckteeth but a giant gap which made them stick straight out; I had headgear (yup, I was that kid!), and two rounds of braces; I had big 90's style glasses; and I couldn't run a mile to save my life! Identity struggles aside, it really is a miracle I made it through elementary and middle school with any confidence at all.

I became really good at making people laugh, so I wouldn't feel like they were laughing at me. I tried to be a funny, over the top person to deflect pain, and I was good at it. In a way it felt like I became two people: The inside me (wounded), and the outside me (large and in charge). Let me tell you, it is exhausting to constantly try to prove to everyone in your life you are worth liking/loving and then living with constant fear that they are going to leave anyway.

So, when did my foundation start to fall in? During middle school I began to crumble. I could go into lots of ugly details here, but the point of the story is not to show you how ugly things got, but to help you understand my identity was misplaced.

In short, I became a cutter, I hurt and abused my body because that self-inflicted pain was more bearable (and controllable) than pain I felt from the stranger that "gave me up." I turned to boys and began serial dating. Not that I dated a lot of people but I always had a boyfriend and their opinion defined me. I even began dabbling in alcohol. Somehow I was trying to find my worth in it all.

At this point I became an expert at being two-faced. I smiled, went to church, and spouted all the right words, but my heart was dying and I literally hated myself. My precious parents did everything they could think of to help me overcome my struggles. In a last "ditch" effort they gave me letters that my birth family had written to me the day they signed the adoption papers.

My parents were waiting to give them to me when I was 16, but they knew I was desperate for identity and worth, so they gave them to me early. It is amazing how much that meant, simply because I had no details until that point. And as I said early, I was striving constantly to find identity from my circumstances (biological family included). Growing up I would create all kinds of different personas for my birthmother. One day she would be superwoman. Her job was to save the world, and knew raising me would keep her from her duties…so she gave me up, but was always close by watching me.

The next day she was a crack addict who had a baby every 9-10 months that she sold for drug money. I was simply one that made it safely to a loving family. The next day she was an exiled queen who gave me away to keep me safe. Some day soon she was coming to get me so I could take my proper place as princess of the kingdom (thanks a lot Disney).

And lots of times she died giving birth to me, making me feel guilty she gave her life for mine. In all my imaginings, I never considered that she was just a scared, confused teenage girl that was a baby herself and wanted me to have a life she knew she could never give me. So, when I read those letters from my birthmother saying she loved me and thought she was doing the best thing by giving me up, it help me accept the facts. I read letters from her mother saying how much she loved me, and even letters from her grandparents telling stories about how they would come to the hospital early and hold me...their first great grandchild.

Getting these letters at first felt like someone was filling the cracks and holes in my foundation. However, the cracks and issues were too deep for this to be a permanent fix. Once I received the letters my curiosity about my birthmother could not be satisfied—I wanted to meet her. After gaining permission from my parents I made contact with my adoption agency. I had always told my parents that one day I hoped to meet her and they always said they would help me, and they stuck by their word.

The meeting at the adoption agency lead to finding my birth mother, which lead to writing letters back and forth, and eventually a meeting. I learned that I had half-siblings: two brothers and a sister. I had always wanted brothers and sisters and now I did! Finally the day arrived, just one year after I received my first letter from my biological mom, my parents and I flew to Arizona to meet with my birth family.

There I was, a nervous 17-year-old, waiting for my defining moment. There was a knock on the door. I opened it and my dad stood there, he said "Amy, I want to introduce you to your birthmother" and stepped to the side. Here was this beautiful woman who I had wanted to know all of my life. She stepped forward and hugged me. I will never forget that hug because she cradled my head like a baby. And it made me think that she was hugging me like she did when I was a newborn baby in the hospital. We talked and cried and talked and cried.

Then I realized I was going to get to meet my siblings. They didn't come to the meeting because they were very young. I was so excited to meet them all. From that meeting our relationship grew. My loving and giving parents would fly me out to see them two times a year. Giving of their time and money to help me feel and grow the bond that I had with my birth family.

However, even though I knew I was loved and wanted—and those twisted stories about who my birth mother was could be dismissed—my foundation was still broken. Yes, meeting my biological family was encouraging, but I learned knowing my biological was not where my identity was found. College came and with it more difficulty. I continued down a destructive path. See, even though I grew up in church and had heard all about God and Jesus, I never believed in Him as Savior or gave the ownership of my life to Him.

After a visit with my birth mom, frustrated by her advice to rethink marrying my current boyfriend and my need "to find God," I boarded the plane to go home. I walked to my seat and sat down next to an eccentric beautiful black woman named, Althea. She looked right at me and said, "Before you even think about marrying that man you better get right with God." I am not kidding. She was right; and as I allowed God to come alive in my life, all of a sudden it was as if all of those places deep inside, the cracks of my shaky foundation began to restore.

Everything I sought to define me was hopeless. From cutting to serial dating, from alcohol to trying to find fulfillment in my biological family. All hopeless. But, God loved me so much that He put a complete stranger in my path. I look back now and can see little places along the way that God tried to reach out to me—the One trying to heal my heart—but I was too busy being wounded to listen.

I spent the rest of that flight praying, crying, and praising God. That day, I found the Savior and Healer of my soul, Jesus Christ. With every fiber of my being I decided that I would belong to Him forever and give over all control to the Master of my life. Only then did I find my true identity, my future, and my eternal Home.

Years of rejection didn't go away overnight. I still fought temptations to believe the lies, but I learned to fight, and to take captive those thoughts and examine them through the lens of Truth. God not only sent His Son to die for me, but also put people in my path to bring me to Him. The more I learned about His love for me, I realized my real worth.

Even now God led me to a friend, who introduced me with Bartow Family Resources, who inspired me to share my story. He is still directing my steps. God has filled me with HOPE, so now I encourage others—grown adopted children and adoptive families—to flourish in Christ as they live their stories.

As I stated from the beginning, my story is *my* story…and my feelings of rejection were rooted in much more than being adopted. But, if you have friends who struggle with their identity—assure them of their value, but most importantly introduce them to the Maker of their souls. He is our Identity. When we allow our beloved Father to adopt us into His family, then we can truly understand who we are! And then we can trust Him that He knows what is best for us…even *who* are to be our parents!

I leave you with Truth.

- I am not unwanted/unloved/deserted: "For God so loved the world, that he gave his only Son, that whoever believes in him should not perish but have eternal life" John 3:16.
- I was not a mistake: "[God] formed my inward parts; [He] knit me together in my mother's womb" Psalm 139:13.
- I am not alone… He is with me always: "He leads me beside still waters.   He restores my soul. He leads me in paths of righteousness for his name's sake" Psalm 23:2-3.
- I am not defined by how I came into the world: "My frame was not hidden from you, when I was being made in secret, intricately woven in the depths of the earth. Your eyes saw my unformed substance; in your book were written, every one of them, the days that were formed for me, when as yet there was none of them" Psalm 139:15-16.

I am an adopted daughter in God's family. Perfectly accepted, perfectly restored, and perfectly CHOSEN. I now have an inheritance as God's heir. And I am the beloved daughter of my God-chosen family.

Birth mothers reading my story please do not let it discourage you from choosing adoption. My birth mother is a hero for giving me the life she couldn't. It was the selfless and best decision for her to make! And potential adoptive couples, don't let the fears of a rebellious child cause you to reconsider adopting a child who needs you. I praise God for my adoption. He made me into the woman I am today...because of my CHOSEN parents!

Adoption has produced in me a heart to understand the vastness of love and see the magnificent plan of God. And, the truth of my story is simple: God is my Identity. Glory to the Father!

A Tribute to Bartow Family Resources

~

*N*one of these stories and miracles would be possible without the incredible volunteers, employees, directors and donors at Bartow Family Resources. In 1989, a group of members from Tabernacle Baptist Church of Cartersville had a vision of helping pregnant ladies in crisis. This ministry grew into what became The Pregnancy Care Center.

In 2002, this ministry became The Women's Resource Center. And finally, in 2012, the present name, Bartow Family Resources fit what is happening at the center. With each name change came more clients to love and care for. We began seeing the men and women flood the doors through our Baby Bucks Program, a parenting education program.

Moms and dads can "purchase" their child diapers, formula and other baby items by simply taking time to educate themselves on how to be better parents. Bartow Family Resources also added a Relationship Center arm to the outreach. The Relationship Center provides free of charge peer counseling, mentoring, Daddy Boot Camp, Adoption Education and support, Jobs for Life ministry in the jail, and many more relationship education courses.

What began in Doctor Mason Brown's office, became housed on the property of Tabernacle Baptist church in two small houses (there was never a charge for rent!), Bartow Family Resources now resides in a beautiful 10,000 square building where our entire ministry can all be under one roof.

The new building was a big step of faith. With community support that step of faith has proven to be a true light for those who champion all stages of life.

The center has now become a pillar in the community, not only offering support to protect the unborn, but also establishing healthy relationships and creating lasting life skills. The center presently serves on average 140 clients per week.

We would like to pay special tribute to all the past and present directors of the center, Andrea Atkins, Judy Bruce, Lina Maxwell, Rebecca Banks, Susan Kennedy, Lynn Tate, Randy Winn McSwain, Kim Lewis, Cindy Smith and Maryland Guthus.

We realize it's more than a job; it's a calling. Thank you for all your time, service and caring…for all the late nights and wee morning hours on call. We thank you!

Thank you especially to all the volunteers who love unconditionally and serve selflessly, whole-heartedly day in and day out to make a difference. We thank you!

On behalf of every family in the book, for every life saved, for every life changed…there are no words to express our gratitude to you all!
—CINDY SMITH

A Note From the Editor

~

*N*ever before has a writing endeavor been so refreshing, challenging, and filled with God's abundant love. Through the thread of Bartow Family Resources, God knit my husband, Dustin and I, with our precious son, Jaden. Cindy Smith, the Director of the Relationship Center was there with us through it all: From the first hopeful meeting at Cracker Barrel expressing our desire to love a child, to the dream-come-true moment at the hospital welcoming our son into our family. Her kindness and friendship continues to bless me beyond words.

As the awe of God's plan and goodness overwhelmed us on that beautiful day, Cindy shared with me her dream of writing this book. Over the last few decades so many extraordinary stories passed through the doors of the pregnancy center, it was time they were shared.

Cindy's desire was to encourage women facing crisis pregnancies to find hope in the stories of these heroic birth moms and loving families. There was another option for these women—abortion or raising the child—were not her only two parenting options.

Cindy also hoped these families' stories would act as a tribute to their CHOSEN children, and to inspire more couples to adopt. Just as God knits families together through biology, He also miraculously entwines us together through adoption. *The Thread* became the perfect title as she considered how God unfolds His plans.

Cindy knew I had a passion for writing; and that I had just published a book, and was working on a second. With my *labor of love* sleeping in my arms, I couldn't resist the opportunity to help Cindy bring life to this book. So, I agreed to be the author/editor for *The Thread*—Cindy's labor of love.

For me, this book wasn't just editing some stories and writing a couple chapters. It was a season of healing and growth. As you read in Chapter Eight, Dustin and I walked the hard, lonely road of the loss of a child and unexplained infertility. If you share our struggle, then you know that no one besides you and your husband truly understand those painful moments.

Reading the stories in this book from couples that also experienced the heartache of empty arms and then seeing God fill them with a precious child was like finding lost friends. Dustin and I are in awe of our amazing son, Jaden. He is the greatest gift God could give to us. Even while dating, we always dreamed of a big family, adoption being a part of that plan. Although there are no physical problems doctors can find, having biological children may or may not be in our future. Only God knows. And even though adoption was always a goal for our family, after the gift of Jaden, we are the most passionate adoption advocates!

These stories helped me grasp anew (witnessing through other couples lives too), that God is after a greater mission than putting families together. He is about uniting the Family of God for eternity! The Word of God makes clear that we are to "be fruitful and multiply" (Gen. 1:28). This is also the Great Commission given by Jesus as He departed from Earth to be with the Father (Matt. 28:18-20). In both passages, God calls us to make worshippers in His image. With that encouragement, I gave God our family. It will be up to Him to fulfill us as a family of three or a family of six, or eight…or…you get the idea!

On a Sunday morning, just weeks before this book was published, Dustin left very early for pastoral duties before meeting up with me and another couple for premarital counseling. As we talked with this young couple, the man decided to surrender his life to Jesus. In that miraculous moment, God created, *through Dustin and I*, a worshipper in His image! Who knows the number of children God will allow us to have, but we know through God's grace, He will use us to lead men and women back to Him, the Father—and they are our spiritual *children*!

I say all this to encourage readers to see a bigger picture. God's plan is to grow families on Earth. But, His greater plan (which I hope you heard while you read) is to call His lost children to Himself, the Father whose arms are full of everlasting love. This is the Greatest Adoption Story. We hope and pray you know your Savior and Lord, Jesus Christ, who paid the price for your adoption; we pray you are marked, CHOSEN.

As an adoptive parent, I can honestly say: If you want a wild adventure that will help you understand God's heart like nothing else on Earth, please adopt! There are many children, infants through teens, who need someone to call "mommy" and "daddy." Set all those fears of adoption aside…they are nothing more than a B-grade, *Lifetime* Movie. The reality is—adopting a son or daughter will leave you amazed at love's depths as you experience your God-given gift! It certainly has been the greatest decision of our lives.

I hope you have been uplifted, challenged, and filled with awe for the magnificent Sovereign God, as you've read this book! Please share these stories of HOPE with someone needing encouraged from the Author of Life.

K.J. Nally

Made in the USA
Charleston, SC
27 December 2015